The Road to You

A ROADMAP TO FOSTER CARE

COURTNEY FILLEBAUM

Contents

I dedicate this book to the God who called me into the world of foster parenting, and the baby boy God used to change me for the better. Little Isaiah* you may never know the impact your life has had on me. I have never grieved a loss like I did yours. This book wouldn't be here if I wasn't changed in your absence. I will never stop loving you. This book is an expression of that love, as I pray it brings many more children and parents together, in the same way God brought you and I together.

*names have been changed to protect the privacy of children and families spoken of in this book

SECTION I

Packing for the Road: Preparing for the Unknown

CHAPTER ONE

Where Are We Going?

I AM GOING TO TAKE you into the world of foster care. I want you to meet some of the children I've met–children who are spending portions of their lives growing up as a child in foster care. I want you to fall in love with the little ones I've fallen in love with. I want you to imagine yourself in the role of a foster parent. I want you to take one more step toward a life that could be waiting for you. This educational piece that includes exploration and consideration could be the ladder that will lead over the wall of questions or fears you may have.

At the time this book was written, there were around four-hundred thousand children in the foster care system in the US.[1] All of these children are in need of a safe, loving family to call their own. The amount of time a child will spend with a foster family varies from days, to months and years, and sometimes turns into forever. Judges, lawyers, social workers, and the biological family's ability to make changes and welcome their children back home will determine the length of stay in foster care for each child. As a foster parent, your ability to meet the child's needs determines the amount of time they will spend with your family. You have the ability to agree to a certain amount of time and, if the child's needs are greater than you are prepared for, you have the power to ask for them to be moved to a new home. Children in foster care are routinely bounced from home to home, I'm sure in part because there are more children than there are families to take them. It is common for a child to stay in four different homes during their first year in care. If the child stays in care until adulthood, they may stay in as many as fifteen different homes. That's different homes, different family rules, and different school systems, not to mention the lack of continuity in care with the people that are meant to represent and protect them. Up to 10% of children in care will spend their time in several different homes and end up having no stable family base to call on as they begin their lives as young adults.[2]

So, here we are with at least 122 million families in the country, and yet there are always children, ages zero to eighteen, sitting in offices and laying in hospitals that don't have a family they can go home to. There are always more children waiting than there are waiting families. The homes that are licensed and considered "open" to foster children are called on more frequently than what they can say yes to. If you are wondering if God could use you in this foster world, the answer is an abounding yes.

A Map Could Help

If you had a map of what it might look like to be a foster parent—where the dangers are, where the fun is, and a list of the things you should pack with you for the journey—would you go? Could you increase the open home total by one? My family and I did. If you think just one more home won't be enough, you're right. But that one home matters to the children and families that have spent time in our home so far, and the ones to come. Your home will house children that mine hasn't housed. You and I cannot be the answer to the whole problem, but we can be part of the solution.

If you are already a foster parent and you know how to get licensed, and what it may entail to be on this journey, feel free to skip ahead to chapter three, and remind yourself why you are where you are. Or go straight to section two, titled "On the Road."

Let's make sure we are all traveling well. You may have picked this book up just to learn about what it looks like to be a foster family. Whatever your reason, I'm so glad you are here. Let's go meet the faces my family and I have held dear and imagine the ones that are waiting for you!

The First Step Is Entering In

When I was a kid and my dad was going somewhere, I pretty much always wanted to go. I knew the trip would be fun because dad was fun. I knew there might be unexpected stops, but dad would make it worth my time because he loved me. Whether that meant there might be a gas station treat, or a stomach-dropping drive over a hill we called "thrill hill," it didn't matter. I knew the guy driving loved me and loved life, and I could always trust him behind the wheel.

There have been times in my adult life when he got my whole family in the van on a Sunday. Next thing you know, the kids are screaming as we take an old, leaky, maroon van through the car wash and find out just how many of us will stay dry while the van gets a good ole shine. This was usually a lot of fun, unless I had an agenda for my day. I would tell my husband (who always wanted to jump in the van), "If we get in there, we could be gone all day. You don't know when he will bring us back!"

The experience of being a foster family is much like an adventure with my dad. Once you get in the van, you never know when the ride will end. However, if you put God behind the wheel, you can trust him. On the other hand if you have an agenda for this experience, fostering children isn't going to be very much fun. You will be anxious and ready to get the ride over with and get on with your day. I encourage you to begin this journey with the mindset of "This will be an adventure. Let's see where we end up."

God Will Use Your Willingness

What does it look like to become a foster parent? Have you heard some crazy things? Maybe you have read or seen some scary things about foster kids and foster parenting. I know I had before we started. People love to tell the "it all went wrong" stories. But what does it really look like to be a foster parent? Am I old enough? Am I too old? Should I have biological kids first? What if I don't have any kids? What if I have young kids at home already? Is it safe? Won't my heart get broken? Will this ruin my life? What if I work full time? What if I'm a homeschool parent?

I don't know what you're asking yourself, but I worried that my kids were too young, my homeschooling would be inhibited, and that adding in one more child would ruin the good things we already had going. If you are asking some of these same questions, the answer is, if God is calling you, there's nothing to fear. He uses the most unlikely, underqualified, and willing. If you are willing, you can be assured there is a role you can fill. Whether you feel led toward teens, sibling sets, babies, or just a role of supporting those who already house children in foster care, God will use your willingness.

Foster Parenting Is Just Life with More Life In It

Foster parenting looks like a regular life with extra levels of highs and lows. The highs are really high and some of the lows are really low, but overall it is a lot like your life. There are good days, there are bad days, and there are in-between days. There are days I wish I didn't agree to so much and days I feel I could take on the world. The only difference for me is that tomorrow might include another child at the table or one less baby in our nursery.

That can be exciting or saddening for those I've chosen to share my heart, home, and family with, depending on the details of the stories being written in their lives.

Foster parenting is an experience not a lot of people choose to have. It's an undiscovered country to many. Some people lose heart while trying to find their way in the foster care world and turn back. I can assure you, at some point you will get tired and question why you came. But the views are so spectacular that some will take your breath away and you will wonder how it is that this gets to be your life. You could look down into a baby crib, or across your dinner table, and there will sit a precious soul that so desperately needed someone to say, "I'm so happy you are here." You will truly be so happy they are there. Your soul will ache at the thought that God may not allow them to stay forever, but you will know that you would never want to have lived any longer without knowing and loving the person you see.

What You Expect Isn't What You Experience

What are you expecting from this experience? What kind of agenda could you or I have, other than to be a vessel of healing to the hurting? I'll speak for myself first. I thought that the first baby placed with us would stay forever. I thought *after* the anticipated adoption, we would probably foster other children. Spoiler alert: that is not the order God had in mind for us.

You may be starting the journey in hopes of adopting like I did, or you have the intent to reunite children with their first families. You may have the desire to keep sibling sets together. (It's estimated that two thirds of the children in foster care have a sibling, and more often than not they are separated from each other during their time in care, if not forever.)[3] To be clear, wanting siblings and first families back together are desirable goals, and they are certainly going to be a big part of your experience in the foster-parenting world. However, if you are only focused on the outcomes you want, it will be hard to see God at work when *what you expect isn't what you experience.*

Inside the foster care system you will witness injustice. Siblings will be separated from one another. Some first families will get what appears to be too many chances, and some first families will be treated too harshly. Sometimes you will say yes to a child and find you don't have the resources to meet the child's needs so you will have to ask for them to be moved to another home. Some children will reach a point of adoption and then a biological relative will step up at the last minute and be given custody of the child you pictured yourself loving and raising forever. You will not be able to control the outcomes. If that last line makes you want to stop reading, I understand. I long for control. I like to see my plans go my way, and yet looking back over the last years fostering, I can still assure you that God's plans are always good. He will not abandon you or the children you love. You may not understand the ways in which he chooses to work, but you can trust him.

You Can Trust God

This fostering world requires you to be full of faith in your God. Believe me, more faith will be developed on the road; however, you need to know who you're placing your trust in before you even begin. If you can't place your hope in something above the decisions of men and women, the world of foster parenting will be a frustrating place to enter and live. You will need faith in God's sovereignty. There will be times you see him at work, and times you don't. You must know deep down in your heart that no matter what you see, God is *always at work!* You will need to remind yourself God is a God of justice, and it's not just you fighting for children. As it says in Isaiah 59:15, "The Lord looked and was displeased that there was no justice."[4]

Your God loves you. He loves the children that are spending part, if not the whole beginning portions, of their lives in the foster care world. God will have everyone's best in mind. You can trust him, and you will *need* to trust him, for this journey.

You can also trust me. My family and I have been fostering children since 2016. I don't know it all, but I know a lot. I am going to share what I've learned so you can go into this experience more prepared than I was when I entered. I want you to love your foster care journey and truly enjoy the ride. If you're ready, I'm ready to share our foster parenting story with you. The little ones we have loved represent the lives of so many other children in their same vulnerable position of need. I've shared my experiences to guide you to and from the children that could be waiting for you as well. I'm an open book. Anything I've done right has been by the grace of God and the guidance shared with me by those who have gone before me. I will share all the things I've done wrong in hope that you can learn from my mistakes. There's nothing God can't redeem, both in the lives of the children we aim to love well, and in the mistakes we make in the day-to-day walking out of the goal to love people well.

CHAPTER TWO

Who's Going?

I OVERHEARD A WOMAN ONCE SAY, "Sometimes my other children don't understand my calling." She was in the process of bringing another child into their family through adoption when she said this. I thought, "This choice affects all of you. Wouldn't it be best for everyone if the whole team was on board before you added another child to the mix?" What child wants to enter a home where some of the children there don't wish for another sibling? I'm sure they will let him or her know their displeasure, as children do. My husband Eric and I have always involved everyone in our house in the decision to bring a child in or not, and still my kids have been known to say things like "Yeah, well that was before I knew he or she would be like *this*." My response was a laugh and an honest "Hey, you think your dad didn't have that same thought after he married me?" We all have our moments of looking back. We need to be able to look back and remember we all said yes at the beginning, and those who said yes to walk into a decision will also be together on the walking through and out.

While I was growing up my dad coached inner city boys' basketball teams. He held camps for his guys, and my mom and my sisters and I were always the behind-the-scenes team with him. We cheered at the games. We made pancake breakfasts and filled water balloons for the water wars at summer camp. We were part of the mission to provide a great time for "dad's guys." I loved being part of that experience. I loved being on the team. I knew then and there I wanted my family to be a team like the one I grew up in.

You need a team. Everyone does. If you are a single parent, you need a community that's going to support you on this road. You need them to lift you up when it's hard, and you need them to love the children that become yours for any period of time. We all need people that will lift us back up when we fall, and bring us dinner when court dates took it all from us. Foster care is an emotional ride.

When Eric and I got married, we hadn't talked about adopting or fostering. I knew he loved children and loved his family, so I married him. As my kids used to say, "Easy peasy, lemon squeezy." He love's God, family, and kids? That's all a girl needs to know when her dream is to be a mom and change the world. However, when it became clear to me that I wanted to start down the road of foster care sooner versus later, I started talking to my husband. He wasn't a flat out no on the options I presented, but he wasn't anywhere close to a yes either. You may have a spouse who has never had foster care cross his or her mind. Give them time to think about it. You absolutely do not want to talk someone into a role they will question at some point. If they feel like you tricked them into foster care, or dragged them like you were playing tug of war, they will say "I told you so" or "this is all your fault" when you reach the inevitable moment of looking back and wondering what you have done. Instead, you need them to be right there beside you, reminding you why you came and where you are headed. It is *essential* that your spouse is on your team.

I believe that God does not call us to do things inside our marriages and families that will rip us apart. If his goal is for families to stick together forever, then why would he call us to jobs and callings that will be the death of our marriages and families? He wouldn't. He doesn't. So, I encourage you to make sure that God is calling you. Also, give him time to call those already living in your house. If he is calling you, he will call them too.

What to do While You Wait on God's Timing

Whether you are waiting on a spouse to hear from God that caring for children in foster care *is* for your family, or waiting until the licensing classes begin, there are many opportunities to wait on the road to becoming a foster family.

It can be hard to accept that God's timing isn't your timing. Trust me, his timing is perfect and he always has your best in mind. In Proverbs 16:9, we are reminded that "In his heart a man plans his course, but the Lord determines his steps." Even if right now isn't the time for you to foster personally, you can support families that are already fostering.

My family put together "welcome bags" for foster children and invited our neighbors and friends to help. We were taking classes to become licensed and this was a way for us to help while we waited for our opportunity to welcome children in foster care into our home. We invited our community to participate because it's more fun when it's a party. We packed duffle bags with a few things that would hopefully be comforting to a child just placed into care. The bags contained a few things, like a blanket and toothbrush for their first night away from home, and could be used to carry their own things if they didn't have a bag already. This was an active way to be part of the fostering world when our family wasn't yet ready to foster.

There are organizations that are already serving children in foster care. Find them and ask how you can support them. We heard of Grace House Ministries in Fairfield, Alabama. We toured a group home and asked how we could support them. They said they needed more welcome baskets for the girls that would join them. We bought the supplies they requested and made baskets. While we were on that tour, they mentioned to my friend they were in desperate need of a teacher for the girls that they schooled on their campus. Next thing you know, my friend was teaching there for a season.

You can also make meals for foster families who have a new child placed with them. You can always be praying for those in care. You can shop for and bring games to the visiting rooms at your local Child Protective Services buildings. Google. Ask around. Take a friend. You'll find your place to fit in and serve the foster care community.

All the while, pray that your family members will change their hearts about foster care. Or ask that God will take the desire from you, or show you other ways to love the children and families in foster care. You need to be obedient to God, but don't do it if that's in direct opposition to the one you're married to or the children you already parent. If God wants your family to do this, then he is more than capable to show himself to all of you. It's not on you to make something happen.

A Family Experience

I've heard many say, "Maybe I'll foster when my kids are older." For us, foster care is a family experience and Eric and I didn't wait for older ages. We became a licensed foster family in the same year I started homeschooling our five-year-old daughter, Kylen. We also had a four-year-old son named Holden, and a two-year-old daughter named Anne Marie. Anne Marie had entered our family through international adoption only a year before. We certainly had our hands full. It didn't seem to be the logical time to add to our family. But during the same week I told

Eric, "We're done, three is it," God gave me a dream of a baby. I knew he was telling me, "No, you aren't done." When God speaks, I aim to listen; especially when it doesn't make sense. I shared the dream with my husband, and told him I thought the dream baby had to be in foster care because how else would we be handed a baby that didn't look like us and was wearing a hospital arm band? He responded with, "What's it hurt to take the foster parent classes?" So before Anne Marie even turned two, we called our local Department of Human Resources (DHR) and were put on the summer roster for foster parent licensing classes. (Throughout this book I will use DHR and CPS interchangeably. In our state, we call the agency DHR, but in many other states this agency would be known as CPS or Child Protective Services.)

Not everyone is going to understand why you would want to be a foster parent. Ideally, your closest family and friends will be supportive and along for the ride. In our case, some of the extended family questioned if we should be doing this. They had just walked the adoption road with us. I would have questioned someone too if I heard that now they were jumping on a new, unknown road, and taking all three little ones with them. Our extended family are a vital part of our lives, and we value their opinions. However, if it doesn't make sense, but Eric and I feel it's where God is leading our family, we will still go forward.

In our case, we wouldn't throw a newborn in the mix without our parents' approval when they were going to need to babysit every week. In fact, just so we could get the nine weeks of foster care classes done, we asked my mom to agree to come weekly and watch our three at home. If she had refused, and if I had not been able to find another sitter, then that would have been a "this isn't the time" answer from God. But mom didn't refuse, and we were able to move toward getting licensed to foster.

In a best-case scenario, your closest people will support you and say they can't wait to be part of the journey. However, they are also the ones who love you most. They will be worried about you. Let them ask questions and take time to think through your answers. You're going to need people who love you and support you. Don't drag them kicking and screaming. At some point, you may be the one needing to be dragged kicking and screaming out of the bushes where you are hiding, eating a sandwich, for a moment of peace. You don't want the whole family out there with you saying, "Why did you do this to us?!" You need them in the house, loving on your kids, saying, "Let mom eat her sandwich in the bushes in peace. She will be okay. She will come back." (Yes, I hid in some bushes to eat a sandwich in peace. This is not a fictional picture by any stretch.)

The journey to becoming a foster parent will require prayer and discernment. You'll need your family to be a team, supporting you in this mission. At times, you'll need the support of your larger community too. Begin praying now about who will be going with you on the journey. You can't travel it alone and you wouldn't want to. There is so much joy in fostering with the ones who love you the most.

CHAPTER THREE

Why Go?

I'VE HEARD IT SAID THAT, "What was hurt in a relationship, can only be healed in a relationship." I didn't know when we started down this road that I would find I had broken places. It's so beautiful that God would heal those places as he allowed me to be part of the healing process for his younger children.

When a child shows up at our doorstep with a hard story (whatever bits we are made privy to), I can't help but see how God brought them to us. He didn't leave them in that hard place, but instead brought them out. He brought them into arms that are aching to hold them and into a house full of faces ready to declare how precious they are, not only to us but also to God. Will he not also bring you out of your hard places? Will he not also surround you with the support you need? Will he not also provide people to speak truths over you when "real life" doesn't *feel* like what is being declared over you? When your future doesn't look bright, but someone looks at you with genuine love in their eyes and assures you that the sky's the limit, that's God. When these little children show up, and you pray and believe the sky's the limit for them, you are doing his work. You go first because you hear God calling you to go.

This venture is more than worth your time. Time is made up of the experiences you have while on the journey. We figured out how to be a foster parent along the way. Love is messy. There isn't a set of rules that you can go by and know that love will make all the endings turn out right. I have wished for those rules. They don't exist. Love is in the moment the phone rings. Love is your heart beating faster. Love is the yes. Love is the first smile of a broken-hearted child. Love is your heart breaking and healing as you smile with them. Love is in the tears. Love is in the knowing and the not knowing where and how your lives will entwine. Love is being there with someone who needs to know that someone, somewhere, cares enough to be in the moment with them today and tomorrow, until who knows when, and maybe even until the very end.

As a foster parent, it doesn't mean that you need to feel love for every child that God ever created. God has specific children that he will place in your home who you are meant to grow and heal alongside. Your love isn't for anyone. It's for *the one* that needs to see their name written on a poster board telling them "You can do it!" They need to see *your* smiling face behind the poster board, holding it up, looking them in the eyes with all the belief in the world that the crappy stuff that's been written down for them, or even by them, up until this point is not who they are as a person. They need your reassurance that their mistakes and hurts are in no way limiting where they will go and how far they will reach when it comes to their dreams and aspirations.

Have you ever had something you wanted to do but were too scared to ask? Maybe date a guy or girl. At our house my dad said, "When you think you're ready to date, come talk to me." Please. You think I was going to do that? No. I waited to see what the next sibling did, and then went forward with what I learned from watching her dating experience play out.

Here I am, offering to be the one who goes first. I'll show you the road, how it has been playing out for me, and then you can go forward onto your road with the faith you can do this. You go because I'm here to tell you this is a worthwhile journey. If I was to start my life over, I would absolutely choose this road again.

I don't want you on the sidelines anymore. I want you to do the thing you are scared to do. There are so many of us that felt just like you. We want you to know that on one hand, you are super special because you are considering this, and on the other hand, there is nothing special about any of us. It's who we serve that we find so special. Because of the children we love, we will work to be who they need us to be, no matter how hard that work is. God is using the most unlikely, boring, scared, weak, and "normal" to serve his hurting children. In the process, the refining is real, and maybe that's why people like to act like we are heroes. Maybe they are seeing the parts of us that are reflecting God, the parts that are shining after the fire refinement. I assure you that we feel like anything but heroes. The kids are the heroes. We are just the fortunate few that get to be right up close to the life-changing action.

Don't you want to be where the action is? I know I do. Especially when it means I will get to be mom to so many more children than I ever wanted to give birth to. I can love a twenty-year-old that lives with her grandparent but still comes to visit me. I can love those in my home that God allows to be a Fillebaum forever. I can also love many, many more that go home, or into other adoptive homes, in ways big and small, known and unknown. That's special. I'm not.

We go on this foster-parenting journey because our God is always going after the little ones who are lost. He does not *need* us to bring about his purpose in the world, because he already sent Jesus for that. However, when he brought Jesus back up into heaven, he left us here to be the hands and feet of the one in the heavenlies. Jesus said if we love him, then we are to feed his sheep, and take care of his lambs.[5] What better place to be obedient than inside the foster system? There many lambs await the knowledge of the love of their Father in heaven, and many also need to experience the love of an earthly mother and father as well.

It's a gift to be used by him. God finds much joy in the lost being found, and if we are co-laborers with our Father in heaven, we too will experience that great joy in the finding. If you read Matthew 18:10-14 you'll find that Jesus says:

See that you do not look down on one of these little ones. For I tell you that their angels in heaven always see the face of my Father in heaven. What do you think? If a man owns a hundred sheep, and one of them wanders away, will he not leave the ninety-nine on the hills and go to look for the one that wandered off? And if he finds it, I tell you the truth, he is happier about that one sheep than about the ninety-nine that did not wander off. In the same way your Father in heaven is not willing that any of these little ones should be lost.

If you find yourself in a position of one who has been found in the flock of ninety-nine, maybe you'll consider leaving *with* the Good Shepherd to go and find the one who is wandering and in need of the safety of a flock.

CHAPTER FOUR

First Steps

THE FIRST TIME I CALLED our local Department of Human Resources and asked how to become a foster parent, I was a mom to Kylen who was three years old and Holden who was two years old. My husband and I were also in the process of adopting a daughter we knew was waiting for us in China. I was volunteering at a week-long summer camp for girls from the area of town where I had grown up. While there, I met a six-year-old girl who suffered from being sexually abused and who was scared of everyone, including me. All the proper people knew about the history of abuse, but as far as I was aware she was still at home. I asked the person on the human resources line, "If she does end up being taken from her home, what do I need to do so that I can say yes to her coming to me?" They said since we were already in an adoption process we were unable to be a resource for her, or anyone else in foster care.

To be the social worker that answers the phone day after day about abuse, neglect, and abandonment, and then have a person who is willing to help but is unqualified due to the adoption process, has to be frustrating too. Every day the kids outnumber the homes that are willing to take them. A social worker has to make call after call and face rejection after rejection when a foster parent says, "I'm unable to assist with this child." As a social worker, you hear horror story after horror story. Coworkers are constantly changing because the caseloads (the number of families/children you are responsible for) are too high. Most social workers don't last very long. Foster parents get frustrated and are calling to find out who the new social worker is, and birth parents are calling to ask why they didn't get their visit this week. Can you imagine? It's not easy for the social workers either. They want to effect change, but there are too many needs to be met, and the resources are never enough.

As for me, I hung up the phone, took the beaded bracelet I wore, walked to my bathroom, and hung the bracelet up on my mirror. During the craft time at camp the girls were given the opportunity to make beaded bracelets. Many of the girls made bracelets for Kylen, but the little girl I had called the DHR about made a bracelet for me. The bracelet that hung from my mirror served as a daily reminder to pray for her protection, her comfort, and her healing. My heart broke for her, and there was nothing I could do to make her life better. I cried for her. I cried because I couldn't do anything. I was a helpless onlooker, and it hurt me to see such pain and be unqualified to join the people in the foster care system that are meant to provide a space for healing, safety, and love to occur.

My next experience with the Department of Human Resources happened when a set of siblings we knew entered into foster care. The night they were to go to their foster care placement (the home that the DHR had deemed safe to place them in while family issues were sorted out), I did the very thing I now do when children are being placed with me. I tried to think of what they would need that first night. I went to the store and bought all sorts of different quick foods and snacks to help that first evening go by more simply.

During the time they were in that foster home, there were Sundays spent playing at the park with our family, and a few times they visited my house and played with my little ones.

Holden had a nickname for one of the girls, and to this day he claims to remember and like her. One Sunday, his buddy seemed to be really struggling being away from her home. She wasn't entering into the games we were playing. She seemed sad. I went to her and let her know that I was sorry she couldn't be at her home, and that it was okay to be sad. I told her to tell me if there was anything I could do to help her feel more at home, and I would get it or do it. I knew some of the snacks she liked and I gave examples. She smiled. I don't remember her saying anything back to me, but she joined the family in the outdoor game after I talked with her.

It's not easy on anyone to be in this world. Not the kids, not the parents, not the social workers, not the foster parents, and not the onlookers. No one likes to watch struggle, and there's much struggle to be witnessed. What's important is getting in the game. If you're not in the game as a player, coach, or water boy, you can't make a difference.

Getting Started with Your Local DHR or CPS

The easy first step is to Google "how to become a foster parent" in your county and state. When I did, there was a foster care inquiry form. I filled out the form, expressing my interest. The appropriate person contacted me and gave me the start dates of the next round of classes. At that point, my husband and I asked to be added to the list. Our classes were once a week at the local Department of Human Resources building downtown.

Nine weeks and thirty-plus hours of classes later, a social worker would conduct home visits to approve the homes of those wishing to foster. Since we were not in a rush, and since I was beginning to homeschool our oldest that fall, we asked to be the last home study. So, although we did the classes over the summer, we were not fully approved and ready to go until December. I say that because if the commitment scares you, know you won't be fostering tomorrow. Even after you are licensed you can say no to the first calls. Getting licensed takes time. You can make up your mind if it's for you as you go through the classes.

The classes included two ladies attempting to paint a picture of what it would be like to be a child in care being moved from home to home with "normal's" that aren't their normal. "Normal" is the term our educator used to describe the environment the child had come from and what they were used to. In that environment they would know the rules, the places or faces of danger, and they would have developed ways in which they were sustaining life inside that normal. The educators had us role play as a foster family who takes in a child and encounters situations we weren't aware of or prepared to handle. Such as, having a child placed in our home that presented with no known behavioral issues, only to find through the child playing Barbies, and acting out sexual acts with the dolls, that the child has in fact been sexually abused. This may be something our family wasn't prepared to deal with. The educators said that when faced with things we didn't know we would be faced with, we could either choose to become educated in those areas, or we could have the child moved to a home that was prepared and equipped to walk out the healing process with that child.

It helped me to hear them say the unknown and unexpected will happen; however, there are paths forward with or without the child you're caring for. I know you can likely look around your social circle and see parents with children born with disabilities, parents walking with biological children who are struggling with addiction, or parents who have unexpectedly lost their children in a tragic accident. You wonder how they can live through that. How do they love that child so well, when loving that child requires so much? I can assure you if they had known on the front end how hard life with this child would be, they wouldn't have signed up for it either. It's only in knowing their child, and loving them with a love a parent can't even really explain, that all the hard becomes *worth it.* It is very hard to love someone you do not know. But once you know them, and love them, it's very hard to say that they are deserving of being let go of, or even worse, never being known.

There were guest speakers, current and past foster parents, telling us about the importance of engaging with the biological parents. They gave us practical tips such as making eye contact, shaking their hand, introducing yourself, greeting them as the parent that they are, and treating them with dignity and not judgment. The speakers said it's scary for the parents too. They constantly feel judged. They may feel ashamed that you can dress their child nicer than they were able to. The speakers opened our eyes to a perspective we had not yet considered. Eric and I were only there for the hurting child; we had not been thinking of how it would feel to be the parent of the child that was taken and placed in our home. By the end of the classes I knew that we were not just there for the children, but their birth families too. I would hope your licensing classes will be just as informative, but if not, maybe your heart and mind will open even wider within the pages of this book.

There was also paperwork. You will have to fill out a financial form (and repeat yearly). This is meant to show the state you have enough money each month to support the possible needs of the children you would add to your home. There will be background checks, written reference letters from people who know you, and questionnaires about who you intend to foster: how many, how old, and why?

Some people may find this too intrusive, but I wasn't bothered by it since we had just experienced similar paperwork on our way to adopting our youngest daughter. I would remind you there has to be a vetting process. How bad foster parents get through is beyond me. The requirements are put in place in hopes of being able to see red flags and protect the children you are supposed to care for. The training and the vetting process isn't about you; it's about the kids you are here to serve. There's not a lot I wouldn't give up or do if it meant that I could be there for a child in need.

You are likely to experience many home visits with a social worker, plenty of phone calls, and lots of paperwork. But at the moment you get to say yes to that first child, nothing up until that point is likely to feel like it was enough. There is no amount of paperwork or requirements that should equal you being allowed to parent a child. Whether you find the requirements useful or not is not so important. The child on the other side of the requirement is the important part.

After you have attended a few classes and filled out paper-work, you will be setting up a home visit with a social worker from DHR. During the home visit they make sure you have a plan if there's a fire, fire ladders if you have upper-level rooms, general order to the house, and living space for the child that you are asking to care for. Oh, and if there are weapons in the home then there are rules for how they are to be locked up for the safety of everyone in the home. Same for the medications in the home. If you get any of it wrong, or forget something on the first visit, they can give you time to correct it and come back for a second visit. A home visit is really not that scary.

Receiving Money from the State

The checks that come are for the child in your home. There's no way that the state could give you enough to provide for the level of care and work you will be putting into caring for children, and then also provide for the needs of the child in your home. The checks are to support their needs. It's not a paycheck for you. In that respect, you will be given enough money.

I have used the check to buy a new and needed highchair, an upgraded car seat (they are expensive!), and other bigger items. I have paid out of pocket to take a brand new young one to their first doctor's checkup. It was only when I got there that I found they were not yet covered by insurance and that the DHR didn't know when they would be. The Medicaid card had not been applied for yet, and I wasn't willing to wait. As a foster mom of a newborn, I needed to know the child in my care was in good health and that someone was officially documenting growth and care.

We were eventually refunded that $160 by the state months and months later because the child's GAL (the guardian ad litem, a court appointed advocate for the child) advocated for us to get it back. However, I paid for the checkup that morning after calling my husband and asking if he was good with paying for it ourselves. I knew that getting money back was dependent on a lot of people putting in paperwork and doing follow-up. Follow-up like that doesn't always happen. But we cared more about the child being cared for than about what it was going to cost us. We do not keep a tally on those expenses. I just make sure we have enough and get approval from Eric first. We won't say yes if we can't afford to. However, we try to use the margin we have for such unexpected expenses. On that day, if we hadn't been willing to use the margin we had, I would have had to go home and wait for the card to arrive before getting the appointment done. This was unacceptable to me because it wasn't the best we could provide for the child, which is all that mattered.

Eric and I have learned along the way that preparing to use extra margin in our budget is a wise way to deal with unacceptable situations. Let me tell you another story. . .

We had a young lady come stay with us while she was between long-term placements. The home she came from had her for several months. When she arrived at our home, her suitcase looked like it came from great-grandma's estate sale. She had no hairbrush, no toothbrush, and the shoes on her feet showed her big toe.

She must have had a hairbrush and toothbrush before. Why hadn't someone made sure they went with her? Let's say that forgetting those brushes was just a mistake. Okay, we can move on.

But why were those shoes the shoes on her feet?! That's *not* okay!

How is she going to feel valued and loved if her feet are not properly covered? Were we supposed to believe that everyone in the family she came from wears their shoes until they fall off their feet? Or were we supposed to believe that no one noticed? That this, too, was an oversight? It's possible . . . *maybe*.

We went shopping for shoes the next day. She wasn't going to bounce around to other homes without shoes she liked that would keep all her toes warm and protected. We were not getting a check to cover her needs while she was with us, as it wasn't the usual placement situation, but it didn't matter. If we had shoes at our house that were in good condition and in her size, we would have offered those. Or if the local store for foster children had some, we would have picked some up for free. But, in this case, we went to the mall and found a buy-one-get-one-half-off sale.

It wasn't ever going to be about the money; it was always about her. How was she going to feel as she walked into new homes with new people, and new schools with new peers? She needn't have any extra reasons to look down on herself, or anything for other children to see and mock about her. Buying those shoes wasn't about spoiling her or providing Disney World. It was about her feeling cared for, and her being able to walk with her head held higher.

For this young lady, we weren't able to meet her needs long term. Compared to the long-term needs that loomed over her, shoes were minimal. We prayed for where she would go and how we could best support her, and in this case, it was shoes. You might be the long-term home for a child, and God might provide someone else to bring the shoes.

I'm not saying any of this is easy. Finances are hard even when you're not a foster family. Adding a child to your home with surprise financial needs will almost certainly stretch your budget. But God provides for his children in big and small ways. It's not all up to you. I wish I could do it all, but I can't. You will probably feel that way too. Just be looking for what you can do and do that. Not more, not less. Use what you have to give what you can, and trust God to supply the rest.

Remember why you are here. Remember the One clothing the flowers in the field, will also give you the resources you need for you and for all the ones you are loving in his name.[6] If he can feed 5,000 with a few fish and loaves, he can make room in your budget for shoes for one of his beloved children.[7] God's blessing will follow you if you are a blessing with what he supplies to you. It's not magic, but it does sometimes feel magical to be the hands he flows through.

CHAPTER FIVE

Are We Ready for This?

"YOU WON'T BE ABLE TO give a baby back." That's what my dad told me when I said we were going to begin fostering babies. I responded with, "They aren't going to give me the option to choose. I'll have to. So I will."

Truly think about that. Are you planning to go into this and adopt, and never have to do reunification? Are you planning to reunify and never have to see a child permanently taken from their family for their own safety and well-being? Are you prepared to be unable to meet the needs of a child and have to ask for them to be moved to another home? What would you do, and how would you handle it, if any of the above are the story you live out instead of the story you are expecting or imagining?

Remember the van rides? Don't go into this with an agenda you're committed to. You need to go into this with hope and expectation, and knowing that God will work in ways that you just don't see coming. He is going to show you that you can do the things you and others think you can't do. He is going to work in you just as much, if not more, than the children you are becoming licensed to care for.

Go ahead and look back and see where God has worked on your behalf in situations you didn't choose. How has he brought good from unexpected places in your past? Remind yourself of his faithfulness then, and know he will continue to be that same God as you move forward in this process. If you will choose to anchor yourself in him, you will be able to do the things ahead that you know not of. You can know that even if what's ahead isn't what you would choose or expect, God will be there with you, and nothing will catch him off guard. I've always been told that being inside the will of God is the safest place to be. It's not because he will protect you from all harm; it's because inside his will you always know that he is with you, he is for you, and you can have hope that in all things he will be given the glory, and he will work them out for your good.

Samaritan Attitude

When we began down this road to fostering, I sought out and read every book I could on foster care. After starting one book, I quickly began to cry and had to stop reading. I said, "I'm not doing this. I can't read these terrible stories. What do I *do* with all of this?" I was already in a season when I felt like I failed my kids daily (as I imagine many parents feel like they do). I got too mad. I wasn't patient enough. I reacted too quickly. I didn't give enough hugs.

Yet, the failures of the adults in the kids' lives I was reading about were much graver. Those kinds of failures left the kids scarred and fighting demons for a lifetime.

Through this reading, and through my own feelings of failure, I was eventually forced to wrestle with this question: Could I trust God enough to give the kids *I would foster* a chance at experiencing a healthy life and healthy family?

You may need to wrestle with that question too. I've found that trust is the antidote to fear. When I find myself fearing if my existing family is going to be ruined, it says to me that I don't think God cares enough to keep them safe. My fear says he will let us all get hurt, and it shows I don't trust him to also bring healing. My fear says that God doesn't care about me, because if he did, why would he let this child I love go home to a place I don't see as fit for them? Fear is a liar. Fear will stop you in your tracks. Fear is not of God. I've experienced plenty of fear in my life and it's never been helpful.

We don't need to know God's plan when we know his love for children is much bigger than anything we can give them. You can know and trust that he wants good for his children. He has a redemptive plan. If you are open to bringing a child into your home, he will be open to letting you be in on seeing his plans unfold.

One Sunday, our pastor was talking about the Good Samaritan, and he said the priest that didn't help had this attitude: How will it affect me if I stop to help?[8] Whereas the Good Samaritan had this attitude: What happens to the injured man if I don't stop to help? Your mind may say, "I'll get too attached. I won't be able to do this." That's the priest's attitude talking. (And if you don't get "too attached" you aren't doing it right.) God loves you and is full of grace for your mistakes and will strengthen you when you are weak and unable to continue in your own strength. God is not the one condemning you. You must think of the children and babies on the other side of your obedience instead of yourself. Think of where they are and who they need at this moment: someone who will fight for a bright future for them. They are waiting on someone who cares for them and believes in them. Do you see yourself opening your door to them? I do.

Aren't your hands full already? Are you asking yourself that? Or are others around you asking you that? I was, and they were. But something inside said, "Well, I just want to be ready *if* there's a child that God plans to send to us in this way." I wasn't taking the classes and getting licensed for every child. I was only getting licensed for the one that he might have written my name beside when he was writing out plans for them and for me. I didn't want to miss that child. I didn't want to find out she or he existed and then say, "I'm not licensed. I can't help." I was afraid I would live with regret if I experienced a desire to begin, but then hadn't been obedient and begun. I knew I could always say no if they called and we weren't ready to say yes at that moment, but I couldn't live knowing that they wouldn't even be able to call me if I didn't first make my home ready and available.

One More Obedient Step

So, I say to you the same thing my husband said to me: "What's it hurt to take the classes?" One more obedient step forward. When you look back at your life, did you always know how it would unfold? Did you always know what was around the corner? Did you always know before you moved? I didn't.

When you show up where God has called you, you'll discover that he has gone ahead of you and prepared the way. He doesn't give us the big picture because we would never believe we would be up to the challenge if He did. He gives us one little piece of the task ahead. As we are faithful in that, another piece is added, and another. One day you'll look back and see a story you couldn't have dreamed up. But if you keep only moving forward in your power, and on your terms, you will not get anything better than what you can create on your own. If you want big, if you want awesome, you have to go where he calls, and trust him for the skillset to do well once you are there. He has never let me down. He won't let you down either.

If you can trust him with this journey, then you're ready.

CHAPTER SIX

What Path Do We Take?

IF YOU USE GOOGLE MAPS, you know how it will pull up multiple routes for the same destination? Well, there are a few routes to foster care as well. Destination: being the one answering the phone and saying yes to welcoming a child in need of a safe place. This destination requires a license. On the way to becoming licensed, however, you can choose to do respite care, be a traditional foster home, or be a therapeutic foster home.

Respite care is temporary care of a child who already has a long-term foster home. This is a great avenue for support of foster children and foster families. You would only have a placement for the amount of time a foster parent needs: a weekend, a week, or something like that. I know some foster families, especially those who are made up of a single parent, that get respite for their child and themselves on a scheduled basis. In that case, you could have the same child for a weekend once a month. This is also something you can provide as a traditional foster parent. In our state the licensing process is the same whether you choose to provide respite care or traditional care. It could vary in your state.

Traditional foster homes consist of a single parent or two-parent home that has adequate space and resources to provide a nurturing and supportive environment for a child in foster care.

Therapeutic foster homes are for children who need a more structured living situation. Some of the children in this category would be better off in a home where they were the sole focus and there wouldn't be other children, or at least no other young children. It would be ideal if it was a two-parent home where one parent could stay home, but I know working single moms who have become therapeutic parents. There are more training hours on the front end, and more training hours required to maintain the license.

The children in these homes may have behavioral issues, special medical needs, diagnoses, or mental abilities that might not be that of their peers. They will need more supportive care than that of their peers. If you feel equipped to meet the needs of a child or children with more difficult beginnings and histories, you may be a good fit for therapeutic parenting.

No matter the route you choose, foster care will be more than you imagine in good ways and in bad. It's no small thing to bring someone into your home and attempt to love them with all you have. Children from places of trauma will likely not know how to give and receive love in typical ways. Their trust has been broken. They have learned to survive in a cruel world. They will still be living in survival mode when they come to your home. They have no reason to believe you will stick with them, or that it's safe to let their guard down. You can't predict or prepare for the ways you will be stretched and changed (for the better if you let it).

Growing Pains

When you do anything for the first time, there will likely be challenges or growing pains. Imagine going to a trampoline park. You're having a great time. You're out there trying to do the things you did when you were twelve and feel like you're doing pretty good. Then the next day you find yourself asking, "Why does everything hurt? When did I even use my side? And since when is there a muscle in my rib cage that can feel incredibly bruised?"

You have foster care "muscles" you don't even know exist. Just like you weren't sore when you jumped on the trampoline every day as a child you will develop strength with the constant exercise of new muscles as a foster parent. They might be weak right now, but they will become something you exercise every day in an attempt to love your child. You are capable of the changes that will need to take place. You are capable of learning new parenting styles. You are capable of so much more than you think you are. When I fall in love and see the hurt, there's nothing I won't try to change about myself if it will help my child be able to feel and know love and experience life in the healthiest form. I'm sure you will find the same is true of you. If it's not, then you will find other ways to support and love from a bit more distance than in your home every day, and that's okay too.

We know a lady who gave her all for her first placement. She advocated for her in the school system. She took her to visits with her biological siblings. She got her on sports teams. She planned a trip for them that only COVID was able to stop, and she took her to the doctors and specialists that were needed. She was an answer to prayers we had been praying for a child we knew and loved, but couldn't care for in our home.

When that child reached the point of adoption, the foster parent knew she wasn't her forever mom. When she signed up to be a foster parent, she planned to be one that was part of reunification with a biological family, or to be a home in the in-between, but not forever. This foster mom said with honesty (which I greatly respect), "I have found that I like being able to do what I want, when I want, more than I realized. After this I'm done."

She realized foster parenting wasn't her forever place of service, yet she committed to stay with that child until she was in her forever home. What she gave of herself for that child's best interest was a sacrifice that she was willing to make. She determined along the way that this was the only child she was willing to do this for. And that's okay!

Be honest with yourself. Be your best. There is a place for you in foster care. What this foster mom did still mattered greatly! What you do will matter greatly as well. You don't need to do everything; you just need to find the place that you are meant to be and serve with all your heart, whether it be through respite, traditional care, therapeutic care, or in some other capacity.

Prepare to Address Trauma

No matter which route you choose, there is not an age limit on trauma. You can limit the ages you'll accept in your home, but there is no age that will put you in the free-and-clear to never have to address trauma. You will need to learn how to parent a child as a trauma-educated parent.

Even if you bring a newborn home from the hospital, that's trauma. That child lost their family of origin and it's going to matter. He or she may have experienced drug or alcohol usage during embryonic growth, or domestic abuse, and there may be tendencies and family struggles further back than you'll know. But guess what? You could give birth to a child tomorrow who one day becomes an addict, an abuser, or a carrier of a life-threatening illness. All of these are things you wouldn't have chosen for the child you grew and loved, yet you'd love them. You'd do everything you could to give them their best chance at life in its healthiest form. You would. That's the kind of parent you are.

Foster care is no different. When the child becomes yours, whether for a short time or forever, you're going to give them all that you have. You will search out resources and you will pray "fighting for you" prayers because they are yours and you are theirs. That's the kind of person you are. The only difference between these two instances is in one you feel like you can choose to not get involved, and in the other you are thrust into the fight without a choice. Weren't these little and big children thrust into these situations without a choice? I have always thought if I get to choose, then there's nothing to choose but yes! If I'm in a fight for my life, then I want to know that someone finds me worth showing up for, and if you are in a fight for your life, then I want to show up for you. By choosing to be a foster parent you are choosing to go into a battle that can find you even if you say no to this foster world.

Pick your path. If you aren't sure which path yet, keep reading, pray about it, and talk to the agencies in your area. See what they need. See where you fit. I know you'll find your spot.

CHAPTER SEVEN

What Car Are We In?
Choosing the Right Agency for Your Family

IF YOU AND I MET and were talking, I would tell you there is much value to be found in choosing your licensing agency carefully. Although you may think that whoever can get you licensed the fastest would be the best option, down the road you may find yourself licensed but desiring more support from the agency you chose. The agency may be unable, or unequipped, to meet that need. It would be wise to find the agency options in your area, and then based on the needs and desires you have for this experience, ask good questions before you choose them as your licensing agency. I would like you to go ahead and consider what your focus and goal is for this foster parent experience.

Every state is going to present different agencies that offer foster care licensing. I'm basing the following sections on the options presented in my home state of Alabama. In many states, you will have the option of a private agency versus a state agency; however, there are states where you will not have this choice. In some states the only choice is the state, and in other states the state will contract out their work to private agencies.[9] No matter what options you are presented within your state, for every option there are children who are in need of a loving home. You can be assured that the pull you feel toward becoming a foster parent will not be hindered by what your state does or does not offer. God will guide you *always*.[10] He is not to be limited.

For the decision process, I recommend doing a quick online search to see what the options are in your state. There are fifty different states so there are fifty different ways that the foster care system is run. If your state provides options, I will help you consider what might be questions to ask, or pros and cons for each option.

Department of Human Resources or Child Protective Services

The state is the one who holds the custody of all the children placed in foster care. The state agency will have licensing classes beginning and ending on a schedule. They have the staff to train new families, and they are motivated to get more foster homes open as they are the ones who see the greatness of the needs. In our state, this was the closest option as it relates to where we would need to drive for licensing classes, and they were the only ones offering classes within a month after I called. I wanted to be part of the team that was the first line of defense when it came to those who can assist the children in foster care in our state. I didn't look any further than our local DHR, and you may not need to either.

Pros:

- They hold the custody of all the children in care.
- They will share the information they know about the child, and the situation from which they come, if they have it and you ask for it.
- They are the first-line responders. If someone comes into care tonight, you could be receiving the call tonight.

- When it comes to resources for fostering and adoption, the social workers are motivated to tell you about them, because they really do want you to be able to care for the children placed into foster care.

Cons:
- The caseload (the number of cases that a social worker is responsible for) for the social workers is usually high, which means in order to do their job they may not be able to respond to your questions or needs in a very timely fashion. Sometimes the social workers spend all day driving across the state to do monthly visits. It's a very taxing job.
- Even when a social worker wants to get you a timely answer, there is a chain of command that they have to go through which can take days, or longer.
- When it comes to resources, there aren't always enough to go around.
- The social worker will be more focused on the child relationship and needs and will be unable to look at your family in a holistic way to assess if all of you are doing well.

Private Non-Christian Agency
These agencies are businesses that asked for approval from their state to operate either in foster care, adoption, or both. Each agency will have a focus that is unique to them. It could be sibling sets being kept together while in care, teens that are aging out and need life-skill training, or maybe even family reunification. Since they are privately funded there may be fees that you wouldn't have incurred at the state level. That is a question you would need to ask.

Pros:

- Social workers will have lower caseloads and will be able to be more relational with you and your family as a whole.
- You have someone looking at your family holistically and helping you decide if a given child is a good fit, versus you being alone to make that decision.
- **They offer** more support. Some agencies even provide therapy for the children in their care.
- It's a smaller network and community. It may feel more like a family atmosphere, especially if they host events for the foster children and their families to attend.

Cons:

- You are adding a middleman between you and the state social worker, which can lead to confusion or misinterpretation of rules or guidelines that need to be followed.
- There may be more home visits if the state social and the agency social worker can't coordinate the monthly visits to be at the same time.
- There may be fees that wouldn't have been incurred at the state level. This is something to ask about during the orientation process (which is free.)

Private Christian Agency

The only difference between this agency, and the private non-Christian agency is the statement of faith. You will find a private Christian agency will also have their unique focuses as it relates to the children in foster care; however, they will also be looking at the fostering experience from a place of faith. This could be life giving, especially when you are choosing to be a foster parent and you are also coming from a place of faith. You will be more assured that you would be able to speak openly with the social workers about faith as it relates to the way you make decisions and care for those in your home. This is not to say that you won't find Christians in every other licensing agency. In my experience you will. God seems to let our paths cross and our hearts connect with like-minded individuals, whether we are seeking it out or not.

Pros:

- More holistic approach to adding to your family. You have someone making sure you are taking care of you, your marriage, the children already in your home, and the child you are adding through foster care.
- You will be able to get in touch with a social worker more easily due to lighter caseloads and more attention to relationships.
- You may find community within the agency and the other families they support, as some agencies host events for their families.

Cons:

- The addition of a middleman can lead to confusion of details or misinformation.
- There may be more home visits if the state social and the agency social worker can't coordinate the monthly visits to be at the same time.
- There may be fees that wouldn't be incurred at the state level, or there may not. It's something you would need to ask about in the orientation process (which is free).

All of that to say, you are absolutely capable of taking the next step forward in your fostering journey. Agencies host orientations that explain the way their program will run, and while there you could ask the questions that are important to you.

Questions to consider:

- How many cases are assigned to each social worker?
- What known resources (therapy, counseling, summer camps, etc.) are available for the kids in our care?
- If there are sibling sets, is there a high priority to keeping them together?
- Will I get calls about children outside of the parameters I will choose, and if so, how am I expected to answer those calls?
- Do you have counseling or therapy available to the children already in our home, or for me, the foster parent? (This wouldn't be a common thing for an agency to provide, but there are agencies that do.)
- When are the next licensing classes available? Is there flexibility for parents who don't work schedules that would allow them to be there together or weekly?
- Will we be allowed to attend court hearings as an advocate for the child in our care?
- Are we able to have open communication with the birth parents?
- Will we be advised if it is unsafe to have open communication with the birth family?
- Are we encouraged or allowed to do visits with the birth family (siblings, parents, aunts, etc.) outside of the visits ordered by the court?
- Do you expect us to be the transport for the child to and from the visits ordered by the court?

- What does the reunification process look like? Will there be overnights before complete return to parent? Will I be involved in the process, such as providing normal schedules from our house to help with the transition back to family?
- If we have had a placement moved, or returned to their family, will the agency be aware and allow us to have time to process the loss, or should we expect that the agency will not know and we could receive calls for new placement immediately?

CHAPTER EIGHT

What Can We Do While We Wait?

Darling did you know that I
I dream about you
Waiting for the look in your eyes
When we meet for the first time
Darling did you know that I
I pray about you
Praying that you will hold on[11]

When I hear these lyrics, I think of the tension that a foster parent feels. The tension that lies in waiting for the call to say yes to the child God has for you. In that time and tension all I suggest you do is pray. Pray for the heart of the child to come. Pray for healing from what they have endured and will endure in the separation from their biological family. Pray for their biological family. Pray for your family to have discernment so you'll know this is your child when you hear about them, and pray that the Holy Spirit will guide your interactions from the first moment to the last moment. Prayer is the answer for while you wait, and then beyond.

Build Your Prayer Muscles

My human side is *so weak*. I can be great on Monday and ready to take on the world. By Tuesday I'm *done*. I'm done with you, me, the cat, and anyone that needs anything from me. Can you relate to one day feeling like this is the road for you, and the next day declaring, "Nope, I certainly need a new road"? How can we be so on fire, and then so burnt out, in such a short period of time? Human nature. We humans can be so weak, so selfish, so entitled, and we can be such quitters. That's when it's time (it's always time) to dial back into the spirit. We need to be constantly calling out for guidance, and the strength the Bible speaks of when it says the Lord "Will renew their strength, they will soar on wings like eagles."[12]

This isn't fairy tale stuff. I've been in hours of disagreement with my husband; he probably remembers what the disagreement was about but I do not. All I know is one night after going in circles, I finally said, "Not another word, unless it's a prayer." We stopped and directed the disagreement to God and begged him to come make the changes we weren't capable of. When we prayed, he came in. He always does. What we couldn't agree on, or make better in three hours, was changed in fifteen minutes when it was in prayer.

Practice prayer as a first response before your first placement. Practice in your relationships with your spouse, kids, work colleagues, and friends. Start strengthening those praying muscles. You will need prayer to be your first response, and not your last resort, especially in the days to come. It's the only way you are going to thrive in foster parenting.

He truly is *the way, the truth, and the life.*[13] You want power? You want a life-change? You want to have fun? It's all in making him the head, and you being along for the ride. He not only knows the way, *He is the way.* He speaks the truth and *His way is full of life!*

Practice Your Answers

While you are in the licensing process, and before your first child ever enters your home, it would be wise to practice your answers. You are going to be asked the same questions and told the same statements in countless different ways:

- Why are you choosing foster care?
- I couldn't [be a foster parent]. I'd get too attached.
- Who is this child?
- Why are they with you?
- Wow, what a good tan she has. (I think this could be a sneaky way to ask why a family doesn't "match" in skin tones.)

People who don't know you are going to ask questions. And people you know will ask questions they shouldn't, thinking they should be privy to more information than you need to give.

- Are these *all* yours?
- Do you have any kids of your own?
- Did their parents just not want them?
- Are their parents not trying to get them back?
- Why was he taken at the hospital?
- What if their parents want them back after "they get their act together?"

  I really don't like this one. Number one, the hope is always that the parent is able to get the child back, and number two, "get your act together" suggests the adult has complete control in the circumstances surrounding them. If a person doesn't have "their act together" it's usually due to lack of a support system, lack of resources, and a general lack of ability at this time in their life. It's not so easy as a simple choice to do well or not do well for themselves or their children.

- Would you adopt him if you could?
- Could you not have kids of your own?
- I just couldn't do this. I would love them like they are mine and not give them back.

These types of questions and statements are going to happen. People are curious. Prepare ahead of time. Role play, even if just in your mind. Think about what you would want to say, otherwise you may say the wrong thing. I opt for openness because my foster children are usually babies so they don't know what's being asked or said. On my best days, I try to educate and have grace for the wording that may be used by curious individuals. They probably don't know what words to use any more than I knew before foster care was part of my life.

For instance, when they ask, "Do you have any of your own?" I respond with, "They are all mine, but if you mean biologically, then yes, my oldest two are biological." I'm kind. I give them the correct word to use and then answer their question.

We once had someone ask how much it cost us to adopt our daughter. I didn't like that at all. You cannot put a price tag on a child. I tried to defer with something like, "It's different depending on what country you adopt from, and travel...." He wouldn't have it. I finally gave him the answer he wanted while saying I would have given so much more, and done so much more, to become her mother, because you cannot put a price tag on a child's life. He heartily agreed, but also thanked me for giving him the number he apparently needed to have. The tone in which he agreed with me showed me that he wasn't coming from a bad place either; he needed numbers to understand things, I guess. I would never have known there wasn't ill intent behind the question if I hadn't continued the conversation with him. I could have said, "Google it." I just didn't. I hadn't role-played that one. If I had said, "Google it," I would have walked away angry, and he may have too. I do believe God gave me the staying power because he knew both of our hearts in that moment. He can do the same for you. Some people will need to be educated, and others will need short answers and for you to move on.

I've come to realize that if someone talks badly of the birth parents of my children, or the countries they came from, I will have a hard time being full of grace. I'm working on it. I love my children with everything in me, so Momma Bear gets involved if any piece of my child seems to be looked down upon. Their birth parents gave them life, they are a part of my children, so I aim to respect them, love them, pray for the best for them, and always speak highly of them. The countries and cultures that are part of my children also hold dear places in my heart. Just because someone doesn't understand the politics, or cultural norms of a society, doesn't mean that there aren't God-fearing, awesome people living in that country and culture. We cannot lump an entire race or country under one stereotype covered umbrella and hate on the people under it. There are moms, dads, grandparents, kids, and babies under that umbrella. They are all real, actual people who have fears and concerns, and believe it or not, they are a lot like you and me. See? Just thinking about things that have been said gets me fired up. I try to remember the words, "Judge not, that ye not be judged."[14]

One time on the Fourth of July, I was sitting with someone who turned over a firework and said, "Oh, it's made in China. That's so sad." I think they meant America should be making more of its own fireworks. However, my child that was born in China was sitting right there, and I am not sad that her country succeeds at making and supplying tons of things to other countries. These are the kinds of comments I cannot reply to at the moment because I will respond in anger. Instead, I usually choose to vent to Eric. He always reminds me that the people aren't saying it out of ill will, but just out of lack of awareness or education. To which I angrily state, "I'm going to inform them!" Thankfully, venting helps me calm down in most cases, and when it doesn't my husband and I discuss whether I, we, or he should talk to the person. I can be the one to have the discussion only *if* I have reached a more kindhearted state.

These things aren't just said by outsiders; the people who love my daughter say them too, and I think it's because they don't think of China and her birth family. They see a family member and it seems to stop there. I'm glad they aren't intentionally speaking ill of *her*, but I also wish they would be intentional in their language around *her place of birth*. I have addressed it when I've not been able to let go of what was said, and other times I have chosen to let it slide.

Prepare yourself for these situations. You can't always attack people. If you do, they will be scared to say anything around you. If you know they love your kids, and they just need a little education as to why some things are not okay to say, then educate. They can take it or leave it. Reaffirm all the things they are doing right, and don't focus only on one slip of the tongue. We have all made mistakes. We all need grace and forgiveness. I have had plenty of "I wish I hadn't said that" experiences. I'm sure you have too. No one is perfect.

I'm not the one to judge the situations and experiences that lead to a birth parent being or feeling unable to care for their child. Neither should anyone else. I'm grateful God is allowing me the gift of raising my children and being mom to them forever. I take the job of fielding questions and protecting their ears and hearts very seriously.

But people don't know what they don't know. A lady literally asked, "So what's wrong with her?" about one of my children! I'm telling you it felt like she started World War III inside of me. I wanted to respond with, "Well let's talk about what's wrong with you and your kids first." I don't remember what I said. It was something to the effect of, "Nothing." I tried to be kind and quickly escaped to the safety of my house. Another person once asked me, "Where'd he come from?" My response was, "Where all babies come from: heaven." These questions can come from neighbors and people in your social circles–those you would expect to be more tactful. So, remind yourself they don't know what they don't know. Educate if you are calm enough to do so in the moment. Give them grace. Come back and educate at a later date if it's family or a close friend. You may need to calm down first.

What can you do while you wait? You can get ready. Practice your answers. Then forgive the people asking those terrible questions and forgive yourself if you respond poorly. If your child is old enough to know what's being said, ask them afterward how you did, and what they would rather you say, if anything. Sometimes you just need to tell people "They are all mine," and then move quickly on with your day, not allowing them to ask follow-up questions. Other times, you can't do that and you have to say, "God makes up families in lots of ways. We are proud and excited he made ours up through the gift of adoption." I walk away and second guess what I've said sometimes. Other times I do well and I'm thankful I had already thought through a response ahead of time.

Ephesians 3:20-21 says, "Now to him who is able to do immeasurably more than all we ask or imagine, according to his power that is at work within us, to him be glory."[15] He is with us, and his power is at work within us. These children are his, first and foremost, just as we are. If we stay close to him, he will not only guide us in our interactions with the children we foster, but also our interactions with the watching world that wants to know how we do what we do, but doesn't know how to ask that in the best way all the time.

I would also like to note that you can come back to this chapter and speak with older children placed with you about the questions that you may be asked with them around, or the questions they may be asked themselves. Discuss what you were considering as your answers with the child, and get their feedback on how it makes him or her feel. You would be wise to prepare your child for these interactions as well.

One example of where I got it wrong would be when we chose to have an eleven-year-old boy added to our lives. Up until that point, any time I took a new child with us to church I would put their given first name and our last name on the ID sticker for nursery or kids' church. I thought that let the adult volunteers know which parents to be looking for, and it protected the privacy of the birth family. I did not think twice before doing the same on this child's sticker. However, I noticed almost immediately that he took another sticker and covered the section on his sticker that showed my last name.

I could have addressed it immediately, but he had handled it his way, and everyone needed to get to kids' church so we could get to ours. However, as soon as church was over, I went to our boy and said, "Hey, I noticed you covered up our last name. Would you like me to get it changed in the system to your last name?" Long story short, I got the sticker changed for every time he was with us after that. I also apologized to him and let him know that I was only trying to protect him from questions. You would be wise to ask an older child from the beginning what they would like you to say or do in situations where you think you have the answer, because they may have a different perspective.

If we are to train ourselves and our older kids to be ready for the uneducated or surprising words of people, I believe in most cases we could take the advice of a man I met who *does love* well.[16] He advises that our first response to a sharp or unkind word from someone is to say to yourself, What is the most generous explanation for what just happened? Could it be that person really doesn't have the language to ask the question that they asked in a better way? Or have they had a bad day and didn't think before they spoke? Second, What is the most realistic reason for their question or statement? They probably come from a place of curiosity and don't mean ill will toward me or my child. Third, What is the most optimistic explanation? This person, once kindly educated, could go on and encounter others like us and never say hurtful phrases or questions to anyone else.

CHAPTER NINE

We Have Travel Confirmation! Now What?

I CAN'T QUIT LOOKING AT MY PHONE. Will today be the day that our new baby comes? We are approved. We have the crib ready. I have baby clothes out. Where is she?

For weeks I kept my phone near me. Every day I wondered, Will today be the day? It was real, the room was ready, and the license was acquired.

I don't know if you have in mind what your first placement will look like, but in my case, it wasn't who I got. I thought she would be a newborn and that she would stay forever. But she was better. And she didn't stay forever. I didn't think "better" and "not forever" could go hand in hand, but she taught me I was wrong. God taught me that through her.

I've learned to be expectant to see God work. It's wise to know what you're not going to do in foster care—who you're not equipped to take in, or the kinds of situations you couldn't provide adequate care for. And it's wise to have in mind what you think you are going to do. However, you are still likely to get calls about children in need that fall outside of the parameters you've set and outside of the dream God's given you. When that happens, pray. Pray about any call that doesn't make you say no immediately. Tell them, "Let me talk to...," your wife/husband/child, or whomever you are traveling this road with; maybe even your school system. Regardless, don't say yes impulsively, but pray instead. They will let you have a few minutes, believe me. Say, "I'll call you back." Pray about it. Think about it. Then if you aren't a no, call them back and tell them so. If you are a no, call them back and tell them so. They will appreciate having an answer to mark down and show to whomever they report to. They will move on in their call list.

Especially with the older kids, the state agencies will be required to have answers from everyone on their call list. At least in our state, the agency must have a no from every open foster home in our county in order to request the child be placed in another county or a group home. They need your "nos." Even if you would rather not answer the phone and say it, they need you to.

My local DHR once called about a child that was outside of the age range we were approved for. The child was also older than we felt equipped to take on at that point. I responded by saying, "We aren't approved for that age." There was silence on the other end of the line. I thought maybe we got disconnected. Then she laughed a little and said, "I guess I need to explain this. I still have to call, even if it's not the age you want." I knew that. I also *hate* saying no to a living breathing child in need. What the caller didn't know was that my response was for me. I needed to hear myself say, "That's not the age we are approved for." I needed to remind myself that I'm not a cold-hearted individual who doesn't care about this little four-year-old girl they are asking me to consider taking. I am a mom, with a lot on my plate, and we set the age parameters so that we can foster in the healthiest way for our entire family.

This is hard stuff. The social workers' responsibility to call and ask person after person about taking in a child, while the child may be waiting in their office, is hard on them too. Then there's me in my home, knowing I have food and a bed, but I just don't personally have the capacity for this specific child and his or her needs. It's all very hard.

No one wants to have to say no, or be told no. We are all just trying to do our jobs. No one is served well, not the child and not our families, if we impulsively say yes to requests we are not prepared to handle. Saying yes to a placement requires prayer and wisdom. Remind yourself why you set the parameters you did when you entered the process, before lots of emotion was involved, and honor those choices.

Listening for *His* Voice

I believe God speaks to us with specifics sometimes. He may have given you very specific things you are looking for in a placement as a way of confirming that it's your placement. Signs, if you will, to know *this is the one.* But it might be helpful to consider other relationships in your life. If you're married, does your spouse check every single box you first imagined? Does your mom? Your best friend? Are there things with each person you would have chosen differently? Yet those people are your people no matter what. Remembering times when God knew what you needed, even when you didn't, might be a way to help you believe in God now for what he has promised; there's no need to limit him because his promise looks a little different than what you imagined. It's like when you fall in love with a book, but then you see the movie version and the main character doesn't look the way you imagined. Some things are just in our imagination, and they can be different in real life and still be true and lovely.

So, to clarify, *God speaks.* When we were in the adoption process for my daughter from China, I felt a spiritual urgency to constantly be ahead of the paperwork. So, I pushed. We filled things out quickly. We did so even when we didn't yet know if she existed. I was constantly ready. Why? I felt like my daughter needed me to be quick. The agency had assured me this was going to take a while and that I didn't need to expect a quick match. My spirit told me a different story. My spirit was right. She was ready, and she was moving along toward me as I was moving along toward her. Only God knew. Only God could have told me. It was indeed a quick match. They prepared us for at least a year-and-a-half wait and instead we were in China meeting our daughter, Anne Marie, within eleven months of beginning the process.

But at the same time, that same God has given me a dream of another little girl I've yet to see. She was newly born, with her hospital bracelet still on, and I knew I would find her in foster care. Yet when we became licensed, the call that my family said yes to was not a call about a baby straight from the hospital. Five years in, I spent a day fasting and praying, telling God I'm so thankful for the way he led me into the world of foster parenting after "the one," only to show me there were others that were also "the one" along the way. I thank him for each one he sends to us, and I say, "This is the dream baby." Because if it weren't for the first dream baby, I wouldn't be holding the miracle dream baby I hold now, or the ones I have held, or the ones to come that I will hold. My dream is unfolding differently than I imagined. God's directions are different than I thought when I heard them the first time, yet he has been so clear each time when he has gently urged, "This is the one." And then we say, "Yes."

I still wait for the call. I've asked God to take away the desire to meet her in case I misinterpreted the dream. He has not taken it. He has made me very content in the seasons I'm continuing to experience without her. I still look for her though. I still wait. He is good like that. He can be so clear, and then seemingly not clear, but very present. I'm at peace with that. I know he is too good, too kind, and too faithful to ever be able to let me down. With or without her, I have him in the lead, and where he goes is the place I aim to be.

How do we know we are on the right path, saying yes to the right things, and no to the things that are someone else's yes? Pray. Prayer is the answer. Pray about each decision. Then make the decision knowing that it will go differently than you expect; be in for whatever comes before you ever say yes. If you can't do that with the information you've got, you can ask for more. If there's peace for you when you pray about this child, then you will be assured that God is with you on the road. If there's no peace, let someone else say yes to this one.

Joy in Prayer

We received a call once about a little one needing to be discharged from the hospital. This little one was smaller than all my newborns, yet was two months old. The little one had been born early and was just now big enough to leave the hospital's care. Our family loves babies. We specialize in fattening them up, cuddling them to no end, and taking a thousand pictures of their every adorable feature and action. We were also in the process of opening a business, homeschooling, writing a book, working a full-time job, and other assorted activities. However, if all this baby needed was to be held, fed, and loved, we felt we were more than capable to do that.

What we were not capable of? *Being flexible for multiple family visits.* I knew that if this little one had siblings and biological parents there might be multiple visits in order for all of the family to see them. At that time, I knew that I couldn't be flexible for a lot of visits, so I asked the DHR worker if there were any siblings that were also in care. She responded with, "This is the only one on this case." By that time, I'd been a foster parent for six years and I knew that her response was not a no. Sounded like one, didn't it? But just because a case may only have one child does not mean there aren't older siblings, in or out of foster care, that the court will decide all need visitation with the baby. So I laughed and said, "Well I know when the baby gets here I could find out there are six siblings that I need to arrange visits with. I won't be able to do that. If this is the only baby, then we can do it. If it's not, then we can't. Will you please talk to the social worker and let me know?" She laughed too. She knew it was true. She said she would check and get back with me.

She never got back with me.

We said prayers for the little one and their family and took joy in knowing that if we were the right family then they would call back. If we weren't, then we took joy in being able to pray for that little one.

You can approach these tough decisions with joy. If you are the part of the answer, great. (Remember you're never the whole answer.) If you're not, also great. Just be open and ready, and God will guide you always. He always has for us and I know that he will for you as well. His promises are for all those who believe in him; they aren't just for a special few. You can trust him.

There are so many children waiting, but they can't all be yours. That's a good thing. Seeing as how you wouldn't be able to "fix" their worlds for them if you had them all, let's just say yes to the ones that we feel him calling us toward. That way, when it's not what we expect, we can know that he does indeed have a plan, even if it's different from ours. He won't say, "Take this one," and then ditch you. He may say, "Take this one," and not show you the whole road, but that's for your good, not detriment. He knows what we are capable of, good and bad. He is with us and working through us. In him nothing is impossible, so make sure you are in him when you say yes. Then you have nothing to fear.

SECTION II

On the Road

CHAPTER TEN

First Stop

IT WAS DECEMBER and we were closing on some land. Hopefully one day we would build a house and have room for kids to explore the woods, ride motorcycles, get really muddy, and be kids. We had plans to go out and play on it when the phone rang. It was someone from the DHR. The lady on the line said she had placement needs for two different newborn boys. I heard her out but told her no. We were waiting on a girl! I just knew it.

I hung up the phone and started to cry. Suddenly I knew of two little boys who were waiting for homes. Things had already happened to them that I wouldn't wish on anyone. I knew they weren't mine to say yes to, but that didn't mean my heart didn't ache to love them. I prayed for them and asked God to put them in perfect places.

Maybe you are planning to be open to whomever God sends along. Maybe you don't plan on ever having to say no to the placement of a child. If you are able to use a private agency, you may be able to limit yourself to only getting calls about children you are prepared to say yes to. Therefore, you don't have to be prepared to say no to as many placements as our family has had to. If you go through the state agency, like our family did, it is highly likely you will receive calls about children that are outside the age you are approved for, in sibling groups bigger than you are prepared for, or with needs you do not feel equipped to meet. Saying no to a child is very hard, but it may be necessary. I say all of this to emphasize that you'll know the child you are to say yes to when the time comes. You can always say no, but when you can't say no you'll know this one is the one(s) meant to be with you.

When we were in the adoption process for our Anne Marie, there was a child's file given to us before we knew of our daughter. My husband immediately knew this wasn't the child we were to say yes to. I knew it too, but it was so incredibly painful to say no. Even though there were medical needs I wasn't equipped to meet, it felt like saying no meant I didn't value that child's life, and I did. I knew I didn't have what it would take to meet that child's needs and that also hurt to admit.

I learned through that experience that even when you know that a baby or child isn't supposed to be in your home, saying no is painful and it takes courage. I have prayed that you will have discernment to know the ones that are to come into your home, and that you will have peace that God has prepared places, for the children that you need to say no to. He may ask you to walk through fire with a child, and if he does, you will want to know that he is in the lead; you said yes because he told you to. I have found myself crying out, "I'll walk through hell with this baby, but you must tell me that's what you are asking me to do first." By making sure God leads, and not your emotions, you equip yourself with his miracle-worker power as you and that child face whatever the future is going to hold. Every decision you make needs to be the right yes, no matter how it turns out.

You may ask, what does the *right yes* look like? The right yes is someone your whole team agrees to. Someone that you all feel you don't want to go the rest of the day without meeting. Someone whom you feel in your gut (where perhaps the Holy Spirit resides), is supposed to be in your home, at least for a time.

Each Family Member Has a Role

Shortly after the call about the little boys, I was in the kitchen when DHR called again. The placement worker (this person's job is to find homes for the children who need a place to stay; they are not the social worker with the details who manages the case) said, "I have a little girl who is six months old. It should be a short placement. Are you interested?" I asked, "How short is short?" I was thinking we could take her while waiting for the call for a long-term newborn girl, right? She said, "Maybe three to six months." That was not exactly short term in my mind. I told her I wanted to talk to my family and I would call her back. I am always in the role of answering the calls, collecting details, and then bringing the information to Eric. When I present the details to him, he will ask questions I perhaps didn't think to ask and I sometimes call back for those answers; but if his questions aren't make-or-break, we go ahead and present the information we have to the next level of our team, the kids. We did not go into this with a plan laid out on who would answer and how we would decide, but this is how it went down with our first call and it became the system we use almost every time. Sometimes Eric isn't home when a call comes, and I will let the kids in on the details while trying to get in touch with Eric; but we make no official decisions (with the exception of one surprise overnight visitor) without the whole team being involved in this way.

You may be the dad who answers the phone and collects details, but be assured there is a role for everyone that feels more natural and that each team member is well equipped to handle. Embrace the differences in personalities and abilities, and seek to encourage and affirm the strengths you see and discover in each person. Those kind actions not only let everyone feel like an important part of the team, but also fuels the passion in each person. Each person will then be able to find joy in what they bring to the team, without feeling guilt or shame that their gift isn't the gift mom, dad, sister, or brother has. We are all uniquely wired and it can be really fun to discover how each person in your family, or in your close community team, will bring something to the fostering experience that no one else does.

The day of our first placement, Eric and I had the kids sit down in the living room. I told them what few details the lady had given me, and I asked that we all pray for this little girl. My son, Holden, who up until this point didn't want another sister, didn't even let us start praying before he said, "Oh yeah, I say yes." I told him we were praying then voting. Eric prayed, "God let us know if we are supposed to take this–," Holden interjected, "This *amazing* baby." We hadn't even met her yet. How did he already know she was amazing? God speaks through our kids *often*, so I started to cry because I realized that I was a yes. Baby girl got a full family thumbs up.

It turns out that one of Holden's giftings is hearing from God and being very passionate and clear on his yeses or his nos. We listen. God gifted him with a love and burning fire for little ones in vulnerable places. Holden has been known to speak things to me, in my moments of frustration or disappointment, that I know are clearly the Lord speaking through him. He has a connection that the rest of us may not be in tune with because we are answering calls, preparing bottles, or painting welcome signs. All the while, Holden is listening and speaking what comes to his mind. His gift has brought children into our home that I didn't feel prepared for or drawn to, but when his passion is hot for someone, I know it's not him, it's God. Holden can be just as cold toward people as he can be hot. God has uniquely wired him in this way. We aim to encourage the heat and train the cold to be a little less harsh sounding.

Let Each Family Member (Team Member) Shine

Our greatest strengths can be our biggest weaknesses, and that's true in all of us. Encourage each person and highlight the strengths, because when operating in those strengths life will flow into you, and with that energy you can also work on strengthening the weaknesses. Don't try to do all the jobs. Allow each person to find their place, ask for help when needed, and switch roles if a role doesn't fit. Our system doesn't have to be your system. Just know that there is a system that will work for your team, and be on the lookout for how each person seems to fit in a space best. One person may want to go ahead and prepare a meal so everyone will be fed on the day of an arrival. Allow them to do that. One person may get out clothes, prep the bed, or draw a welcome sign for the bedroom door. One may entertain the younger children in the house while the other preps for the incoming child. There are many ways this can work and work well. Just don't let one person run around doing it all and feeling crazy. There may be an encourager and peacemaker among you, and you can tell them to use their gift to help out those of us who are more high-strung and tend to get lost in some unimportant details.

Our first baby-love was a 15 lb., pajama-wearing, white-headbanded, bow in-her-hair, baby *angel*. She was tiny, smiley, and oh so sweet! We were in love with her the moment we saw her. Holden said, "Are you sure we can't keep her forever?"

When I unpacked the bag her mom had packed for her, I was immediately under the impression that this momma loved her baby. It seemed like she packed everything the baby owned. There were bows, creams, clothes, a snowsuit (we live in Alabama and this item is rare for anyone to have. However, it snowed while she was with us! The snow suit was put to good use), and shoes.

That night, I held her and sang "Jesus Loves Me" and then put her in bed. I tossed and turned, constantly checking on her. I was used to kids that didn't sleep through the night at six months old. She slept twelve hours without a peep.

By the afternoon, I was sure God had given us the easiest, most perfect child on the planet in this sweet girl. I had agreed to giving the mom my number so she could call and check on her baby, and she called the first day. She told me a chunk of her heart left with her baby. I could tell that her mom loved her. I assured her that I knew this girl was loved just by the way her things were packed. Her mom told me how smart her baby was, and I agreed. I told her I would send her pictures and that I would tell Angel Baby (the nickname I'll use going forward) that her momma loved her every day. I said we would take good care of her until she could get back home.

At dinner the emotions of it all hit me and I told my husband I was so overwhelmed. He questioned, "By her?!" I looked over, through my tears, where she was quietly sitting on the carpeted floor chewing on a toy. I laughed. It didn't seem like it could be her fault. He said to me, "This is fun!"

My husband is the best. So often I get lost in emotion and he has to speak the stabilizing truth over me and our family, and remind us what God put us on the planet to do. God gave me the most perfect person to walk this path with, for sure. I'm on fire, raring to go, and he is there to let me be on fire, but maybe put a surrounding circle of water on the ground so I don't start wildfires that are hard to put out.

Eric's role on the team is to contain my passion sometimes, and encourage it other times. He asks questions I don't think of. He even feeds bottles to babies in the middle of the night. He is like a big oak tree for us. He provides shade from the heat. He provides a barrier from the fire that Holden and I seem to carry, and he brings cool and calm to our home. He is also the fun guy, providing things to do, and cuddling all our little, snuggly children when I'm out of strength and cuddles from a long day at home meeting the needs of our people.

Our Anne Marie has been a proven provider of imaginary play with littles, and Kylen found a spot on the welcome committee with a camera and welcome signs. When placements end, Kylen excels at sending love along with a child. She does sketched portraits of the little love that is leaving, and writes a note expressing her love to whomever is on the receiving end of the child's move. I'm always surprised when God adds to our forever team and we find that our new addition has another role in this baby-loving family. God is so cool. He has surrounded us with just the right people and I know he will do the same for you. Let each family member shine, don't try to place the roles upon them; just let it unfold and see who excels where. You will all have a lot of fun.

If you're going to be a single parent, involve your friends. Let them bring food. Let them put together a welcome basket for the new addition. I promise God will provide for you and for your new addition and he won't leave everything up to you. You will have so much fun seeing how those already in your life, and new ones God will bring along, will fuel the passion in you by the way they love you and those you welcome in. Pray for God to build the team. He will.

If God is calling your family to this, I promise each of you will be gifted in different areas, with each person having giftings that add value to the whole team. As a team you will be able to love, in a whole and healthy way, the ones that you are called to bring home, whether that be for a season or for a lifetime.

She was here. She was amazing. The first stop was exactly as it should have been, even though it looked different than the newborn I had been expecting.

CHAPTER ELEVEN

Overlooks

AN OVERLOOK IS A SCENIC SPOT along a roadway where you can stop your car and look around. Maybe you see a bird's eye view of what's ahead, or you look back to see how far you've come. The overlook is a place to stop and observe. I see court days and ISPs as days where you get an "overlook moment." (ISPs are Individualized Service Plan meetings. In these meetings the social worker, guardian ad litem [GAL] for the child, the foster parents, and the biological parents all sit around a table and sign off on the "where we are headed and how we will get there" plan.) In the day-to-day caring for a child, you can be very much in the present without a lot of thought to what may be ahead or near. When you have a court hearing and ISPs, it brings everything to the top. And for me it can bring the peace to a stop.

I see birth parents, I hear talk of reunification, I see the social workers still writing "reunification with parents" as the goal, while at the same time hearing maybe the police were called at home for domestic violence, again, a drug test wasn't taken or wasn't clean, a sibling was moved to another foster home, or maybe the child's social worker has quit or moved on to a different job and the new one is yet to be assigned.

My what-ifs start piling up! I start feeling scared. I wasn't scared when I was at home feeding that little love a bottle and hearing their coos, but now I am scared of the future for him or her. It's looking really bleak ahead. What do you do in those moments and on those days? Start by reminding yourself of who your God is. He is all knowing, all powerful, and he is in fact still here in this moment. He is in the courtroom. He is in the meeting room. The future is never bleak if we believe that whether all of this works out or not, is in his hands. Does this child not belong to him? Does he not care for this child more than you do? Is he not the one who breathed life into this child before you ever knew they existed? He formed "my" baby. He formed you. He formed the biological family and his plans for all of us are good. If only we choose him. It is not easy to see what God is doing sometimes, but I can assure he is still good.

I don't know how my story as a foster parent will end, but I know I'm following God, so it will be worth everything sacrificed and experienced. There are days that it's harder to *feel* that truth, but feelings lie. Just because I can't feel or see how this present moment can be good, doesn't mean there isn't good to be found in it.

In your overlook moments, stop and take a breath. Look back to God's faithfulness up until this point. Look beside you, and know he is right there holding your hand. If looking forward scares you, if you don't like what you see ahead, or if the future seems foggy and unclear. Know that God never changes. He is the same, yesterday, today, and tomorrow.[17] Has he delivered you before? He can deliver you again. Did you heal your broken heart before? He can heal it again. You can continue to walk forward boldly.

Getting Along with Birth Parents

On one visit day, I packed a diaper bag with formula pre-measured to the amount our foster son, who we will call Isaiah, was used to being given, a bottle with water ready for formula, diapers, wipes, extra clothes, and a note with a picture of him for his mom.

Sending "your" baby with someone you don't know, to a situation you don't know, and to be with a parent you don't know is *hard*. My stomach hurt, and I counted the hours until he came back. I wondered if he ate, and if he was okay, or upset. Would mom know how to calm him down? Would she hold his bottle up enough so he wouldn't gulp air? Would she mix it right? These are all the things a parent worries about when leaving their child with someone. But in that situation, it truly wasn't my kid–it's her kid! It was really hard for my mind to comprehend. It may be hard for you as well. We can do hard things. I'm living proof, and there are many, many others who will testify to the same. You can do hard things. They will feel hard. They will be hard. But you will be able to do what needs to be done in order to be there for the child who needs you.

I have an innate desire to find goodness in the birth parents. God used them to create the child I love, so I know good is to be found in the birth parents. I was always eager to write down any good things I discovered about Isaiah's mom, so I could tell him in the future. Whether he stayed or not, I wanted him to know she loved him, and then have tangible proof that would show him the ways I felt like she tried to show him love. On this particular visit, she sent him back in a new outfit with nice, new shoes.

I always tried to dress him nicely for his visit in case she took pictures with him. Plus, I wanted him to be his best self for her so she could see what a handsome boy she had. She would send him back wearing what she considered his best self and sometimes I felt...perhaps, insulted? Jealous? I'm not sure. I just knew I didn't like what I felt. Looking back, I think it was her doing the exact thing I was doing–dressing him as the cutest, most handsome boy in the world. However, then, it felt less than desirable.

Here I was changing the dirty diapers, doing the nighttime feedings, and calming the crying baby, and she would send what I dressed him in crumpled in the side of the bag with his new stuff on instead. It felt dismissive. But again, this wasn't about me. It was about him, and it was good that his mom brought him new things to show her care. I chose to place my focus there, in that goodness, by documenting it for Isaiah in his baby book. I would ask you to consider choosing a new narrative or perspective, if you feel hurt when you give your all and it seems to go unrecognized or is dismissed.

Isaiah had a small surgery during the summer he was with us, and the night before the social worker told me his mom would be at the hospital. I was so nervous! I was going early in the morning by myself, I would be meeting her for the first time, and we would be spending half a day together in a hospital room, alone! I was not excited about facing this by myself, but there was nothing I could do. Again, this was her child.

I got to the hospital at 5 a.m. and was constantly looking around for his mom. When we (Isaiah and I) got called back to his room, I told the nurse that his biological mom said she was coming, but I'd never met her. I felt someone needed to know she and I weren't friends yet, so they would check on us. They needed a written consent from mom in order to do the surgery, so we were all waiting on her. I gave them mom's number, they called her, and she gave verbal consent and said she was on her way.

I walked and sang to Isaiah while we waited for the staff to come to take him back for his surgery. He couldn't eat so I was hoping they would come soon. Right as the OR nurse showed up and said it was time to go back, mom walked in. I handed over the now mad and hungry Isaiah. We all walked together as she got to carry him back to the doors leading to the operating room.

The night before I was worried about how the hand off would go. I wanted to be able to carry him back myself, as I was typically his comfort person. However, when the time came, the hand off felt natural. I walked along beside Isaiah and his mom and answered questions for the nurse.

I planned to use the time during surgery to get to know about mom's time with Isaiah. But at first, she was on the phone with Isaiah's dad. When she hung up, I took the opportunity to ask her how it was being pregnant with her son. Who chose his name? Did she get to spend time with him in the hospital? Was dad there? What's the first thing she thought when she looked at him? I didn't bombard her with questions, but just know I had a list in my head going into this opportunity for time with her. I worked in any and all questions so that I could find answers for future Isaiah, and also learn about his mom and how she came to be where she was in life.

In answer to the question, "What did you think when you first saw him?" she said quietly, "Thankful." I said, "Me too." Here we were, in a moment, just two moms loving and feeling grateful for the same little baby boy. It was a good moment, albeit sad, seeing as I was the one who would carry him home and she was the one leaving with empty arms. In the search for commonality, you'll find joy and sadness, giving and loss, all side by side. It seems that the good and the hard hold hands.

As the hours passed, I shared with Isaiah's mom the things my family loved about Isaiah. I told her how I had read that morning that good and perfect gifts come from above.[18] I told her that her son was most certainly a very good and perfect gift. I told her how grateful we were to be in his life, and that we were praying for her. She nodded up and down. She wasn't good at making eye contact but she talked freely once she got going. She told me about her childhood and the birth of her other kids. Where they were. How she got here.

It was a hard story. I told her I was sorry those things had happened to her. I asked her if it was hard to tell me these things. She acted as if it wasn't–like she was disconnected from the traumatic events she was telling me about. I just let her speak. I was so grateful for this opportunity to have so much time with her. It was the opposite feeling from the night before. The 3-a.m.-I-can't-sleep-I'll-read-my-bible and-calm-down treatment had obviously done wonders for my perspective of this situation.

The time spent with Isaiah's birth mom was an overlook moment. It brought me out of my day-to-day and into how much this beautiful young lady had gone through and was still going through. It let me see again that this fostering life isn't about me. It's about this child and everyone he comes with. It's about God's pursuit of his mom, God's pursuit of this little son, and God's pursuit of me. God has a much bigger picture than you or I will ever know about.

Thank God for the overlooks he sends you, even when you wish you could get to a different spot than the one you're at. It's amazing how an overlook will put into perspective that you don't need to know the how, or the when; you just need to enjoy the view, make the most of where you are, and trust him with all the hard things that we cannot possibly make the best decisions about. If we were in charge, we would choose the option where our heart doesn't get broken, this child never faces hardship, and that birth parent would probably have to deal with the bad choices they have made on their own "because they are an adult now." God is kind, full of grace, so forgiving, and he knows who can handle the heartbreak and who can't. He knows how hardship can be endured. He knows what we don't know, and that we can come out the other side of this experience stronger, wiser, and better than we ever would have been without it.

God knows everything. He loves all of us. Sometimes an overlook moment is just what we need to see just how big this whole situation is, and just how small we are. Let's not get confused about the size of our role. God will always be the hero. We will always be a major subplot to the whole story, and truly that is such a relief. Let God be God, and you just love those he allows in your life as best as you can, for as long as you can.

Them's Fightin' Words

I was lied about in an ISP meeting one day. The mom said I hadn't sent food or bottles to the visits. She complained that she wasn't getting the visits she wanted, yet I was able to visit with her children whenever I wanted. She complained that the baby had a rash that was from my lack of proper care. I was so mad, but I didn't say anything back. It really helped that this meeting was over the phone, otherwise she would have seen the anger on my face.

Do you know which part wasn't a lie? The rash. This baby got a terrible diaper rash *the day of the visit*. I had sat in my car pouring tears, knowing that if I saw that rash on my baby I would be so mad. I knew what his mom was going to think. Yet there was nothing I could do about it. I still cry when I think about that. One bad diaper found in the morning can be all it takes for a bottom to be red and irritated. That's what had happened. It wasn't a lack of care. It was bad timing of sleep and a bowel movement. I had been right when I cried about it, because there she was, months or maybe even a *year* later, bringing it up! The *one time* I sent him to a visit with a diaper rash. I could have argued my case, but I didn't.

What was I doing the very day of this call? I was driving one of her children over an hour and a half away so that the youngest group of her children could all be together at a school sporting event. I wasn't doing that for me, I was doing that for her children. Yet she lied about me.

It was an overlook moment. Her lies weren't about me. The end was drawing near. She was scared and she was grasping at straws. That overlook view was very sad, but it enabled me to keep my mouth shut.

I let the social workers respond. I didn't say a word. At the end of the meeting, they said the plan was being changed to adoption by foster parents instead of reunification with biological family. The social worker also outlined a number of visits that were even less than the biological family had been getting. Did everyone sign off on that? Yes. One of the case workers said that my husband and I were getting this child all the services he needed, that he was in great health, and happy. This worker said the words about me that were true. My blood was still hot from the lie though. Just because you know why someone is lashing out at you doesn't mean it won't hurt, especially when you have beat yourself up for the diaper rash already.

I hung up. I coped the way I cope on a road trip. I turned on my "them's fightin' words" playlist. It has all my favorite "God is fighting for you" songs in one spot. Then I switched to YouTube music and the good Lord in heaven played a new one for me: "Help Is On the Way" by TobyMac. One of the lines is, "He is rolling up his sleeves again."[19] That was exactly the visual I needed. I needed someone with actual power to be rolling up their sleeves for my foster son, for his siblings, and even for me.

In this world, you will be lied about and even your smallest misstep or mistake will be called to your attention. Every time I would take one of the young ones to visit an older sibling, I got a "where'd this scratch come from?" I knew the sibling just wanted to keep her brother safe, but don't you know if he fell and had a bruise I would think, "how many days until we see his sister? Going to have to remember where this injury came from."

Not everyone will love you no matter how hard you work to do a wonderful job for the child(ren) in your home. People will question your motives. They will make things up. They will get your blood boiling. Just know that the God of the universe is for justice. He rolls up his sleeves. (I'm not sure his sleeves are ever unrolled actually.) He works on your behalf behind the scenes *all the time*. You do not need to fight. In most cases you only need to love the children placed with you, tell the truth when you are called on in court, and allow God to do every other thing.

The place my family and I fight the most is in prayer. We pray for what we believe is best for our children and their families, and we trust God with the details. Sometimes what we want is not what God is going to do. That's okay. God gets to choose if he answers us or does something different. It's okay for us to tell him what we are thinking. He knows what we are thinking anyway, so why not voice it? We know God's plans are always higher and we choose to trust him when we don't understand. Truly, there's no way to survive in situations where you are dealing with innocent children and hurting families without prayer. What do you do if you don't believe in a God that can take death and make life? Can take ashes and bring about beauty?[20] You need that God. You need him on your side, and on your child's side. You need to know he can work miracles because you are going to be in need of a whole lot of miracles.

Sometimes you're too close to a situation to get a big picture of what's going on. Pull over. Look around and see if maybe you just need to be reminded that this isn't about you. You may need to be reminded that God's picture is really big and that his plan is always good. Then you can get back to being in the moment, and loving whomever you've been assigned to love at this point of the journey.

But even an overlook can't show it all. There's always a mountain you can't see past, or a valley you can't see the end of. You have to be holding tightly to the hand of the one who created it all, trusting him with the whole journey.

CHAPTER TWELVE

Deserts: Why Did I Come Out Here?!

I WAS LITERALLY SHAKING AND PRAYING OUT LOUD. Something hit the bottom of my rental car, and I was pretty sure a six-foot-tall cactus scraped all down the side of my door. Four days prior it had been a sparkly new car. Suddenly there was at least one dent and a *lot* of scratches. This was not good.

It was 4 a.m., and I didn't have starry night views at home like the ones that were right outside the windows that night in California, so I couldn't help myself. It was the one night I had in the desert on that trip. Why wouldn't I go out and try to find the best starry night view? Right?! But then I was literally lost in the desert and I wasn't sure how to get back to the paved road. If I blew out a tire, who would come find me? I saw the signs that said, "Watch out for desert wildlife." So, I couldn't just walk back to the road. Even if I did, no one was out driving yet! I tried to stay on the marked path, but it was dark and I was lost. I was worried and scared, and I knew this was all my fault.

Think of a time you made a decision—maybe for a good reason, not wanting to waste another second not doing what you wanted to do—but suddenly you were lost and it was scary! What do we do? Was the choice wrong? If so, it's too late. The only choice we have is to pause and assess the situation. Take a deep breath. Why did we come out here? Have we gotten what we aimed for? Is it time to turn around and find the paved road again? Maybe so. Let's look at our map.

On mine there was a literal blue arrow pointing back to the road, but the way in between was filled with sand and cacti. I had to follow the path left by vehicles larger than mine, and it was extremely dark. I was visiting an International Dark Sky Community, so the light of the stars and the scratched-up rental were all I had. The other problem was that there had been a lot of vehicles out there, just as you have a lot of people around you. There are other foster families, friends, and family, and everyone thinks the path they are taking is the path you should take. You thought you were following a path that was well trodden and safe, but here you are lost in the dark, alone, and not sure of the path back home.

When I was younger, the neighborhood I lived in was a rough place. It was New Year's Day and there was a sewer issue. I was in the backyard with my dad as he dug a trench to get to the problem. Suddenly there were gunshots across the road. My dad ran toward the front yard to see who was shooting and who was being shot at. Being young and interested, I followed. When Dad tells the story he says he was looking over the fence and felt someone crawling up the fence beside him. He says he whispered fiercely, "Courtney, get in the house!"

I thought if he was going, then it must be safe. If he wasn't worried, then I shouldn't be worried. We weren't the same person though. I was a little girl, he was a grown man. He knew things that I didn't know. That's the thing about thinking if your friend is fostering three children you should be able to foster three; or, if your friend is fostering teens, you should be fostering teens. Perhaps you think if you're in it for the right reasons then you should be open to everyone.

There's a path that's marked out for them, and there's a path that's marked out for you. Don't get lost on someone else's path. You need to listen closely to what the voice in your heart says.

Don't follow a path that you weren't made for. If you have a spouse or child(ren) already in your home, you all need to agree to the path you will choose. You will need everyone on board, because there will be moments for each of you when you just don't see the way forward. You need to know you are in it together, and if someone needs to be carried out then the team needs to be ready and willing to carry them out.

I needed to be carried once. This wasn't a rolled-ankle carry; this was a dead-man's carry. The problem was that no one knew it. I didn't know how to put words together to ask for the help I needed. They didn't know how to help me even if they saw something was off.

Lost in the Dark

I had to ask for our baby Isaiah, of almost one year, to be moved to another foster home. In the days, weeks, and months that followed Isaiah's leaving, I had promised myself we would do cannonballs, play, and try to enjoy just the three bigger kids again. The kids seemed to do well with that plan. I, on the other hand, had to dry a face wet from tears and wipe away snot before coming out to greet the day. I was struggling. I was trying to hold onto the promise of God's goodness, but I was feeling guilt and shame instead. I wouldn't let go of the belief that this was all supposed to end differently and the only reason it hadn't were my weaknesses. I didn't think DHR would ever call again, because surely, they felt I was unfit to parent. I took up learning to skateboard, because if you don't know how to skateboard, and try to learn as an adult, all you can do is concentrate on not falling off. If you concentrate on not falling off the skateboard, you can't think about how you weren't enough of a mom to keep a sweet little boy for as long as he needed you. Maybe an unusual coping strategy, but it worked for me.

I'm very grateful to friends who met me at the park and let me talk through what I couldn't make sense of. I'm grateful to my husband for not letting me stay in my closet and cry an unhealthy amount. I'm grateful for three awesome kids who gave me a reason to get up every single day, despite my desire to stay in bed and never, ever come out. I was going through the motions while hoping someone noticed and pulled me out of my hole. No one did. How could they not see I was drowning right in front of them? I pushed kids on swings, I smiled, all while in my head I was in another sad, dark world all alone.

I cannot empathize enough with those who have experienced depression. I understand now. Life seems dull and meaningless. Everyone around you seems like their life is in color and yours is gray. I hung onto scriptures, songs, and messages, trying to climb out of the darkness. I wanted the old hopeful version of myself back, but it seemed I would never find her again. I was able to enjoy holidays and family celebrations, but the brokenness and sadness was enveloping me like a big heavy blanket at the same time.

This is the hard part of the story I feel I have to write. If I don't, then how will God use it to encourage you to keep moving if something like this is part of your story? I never thought I could be the person you're about to meet. But now, I am grateful to know this version of me. I'm grateful that I came through. I'm grateful God showed me my limits. I'm grateful he has already allowed me to share this story in person to help others who have lost dreams, and find the darkness and fear so heavy they can't move. I've been able to truly understand where they were, and confidently tell them my own version of, "This too will pass." I'm not scared for them and their families, because I know if they trust the God I trust, they will find that if they make themselves get up, eat breakfast (you have to make yourself do that), take one step at a time until bedtime, and repeat it the next day, you will find yourself moving when it feels impossible to move.

You have to tell yourself the things that feel untrue, like God being good and kind, and having good plans for you, even in this. Repeat. Repeat. We don't have to understand the why in order to get up, eat breakfast, tell ourselves of God's goodness, cry out for help, and then do the same thing the next day. You may not get an answer to your why for a long time, but that doesn't mean God isn't there or that he isn't leading you somewhere good. He is always leading us somewhere good. Always.

If you are a foster or adoptive parent for any amount of time, there are going to be pieces of the journey you do not understand. There will be pieces you do not enjoy or wish to experience. This is true in every human life. No one goes through the earthly experience unscathed by the brokenness that lives here. You are going to get scratched by a six-foot-tall cactus sometimes. But the views out here are unbelievable. The lack of light in this world of hurt makes the light in the eyes of these children like stars in an ink-black sky. You can't help but get out amongst the cacti, just to let the light in their eyes take your breath away.

I don't regret getting lost in the desert at 4 a.m., and I don't regret saying yes to Isaiah or eventually asking for him to be moved. I had reached the end of my path with him. It was an ending I hadn't seen coming. I had my breath stolen by the beauty of loving him, and then had the wind knocked out of me when I realized I wasn't his whole answer, and I would have to let go.

CHAPTER THIRTEEN

Cliff's Kill

WITH ISAIAH, THE YES WAS EASY. It was a regular afternoon, me sitting in the driveway watching all three of my kids get covered in paint and chalk. Isaiah was three days old and in need of a home. We delighted in his presence. We hugged, fed, cuddled, kissed, and loved him with everything we had from his third day of life to the day he left our home.

However, as he got closer and closer to a year old, there were some milestones he wasn't hitting. I was aware of a group of therapists that would do treatment at our home, for free, if he qualified. I called them. He was evaluated for physical therapy and occupational therapy treatments. He qualified. Now we had two different therapists coming once a month, the social worker coming once a month, a visit he was picked up for once a week, court every three months, and I was trying to homeschool the bigger two kids. The social worker later told me the therapy at home needed to be done at DHR so mom could join us. Oh, and Anne Marie was seeing a speech therapist, outpatient, once a week as well. Home life was getting a little hectic.

On top of all of this, little Isaiah was able to pitch a fit like no other when he was mad. It was hard to figure out what would set him off. Sometimes, he was eating and then all the sudden he was screaming. Sometimes he was playing and then all the sudden he was screaming. When Eric was home, we could tag team him, and he was much better. Maybe it just felt that way because I had help.

I began feeling like I wasn't meeting Isaiah's needs in the way he needed because he seemed to be mad at me more and more. I tried to do anything and everything to keep him happy. He loved being outside, so if he was having a hard day, I would load everyone up and we would go to the park. One day he was so upset and I was desperate, but it was too cold to go outside, so I brought the outdoor baby swing inside. I attached it to the beam in our living room and turned on planet earth. It worked for about three minutes. He wasn't fooled.

Every day I felt like I failed him. When he was screaming and I couldn't calm him down, it felt like personal failure. I would get mad with him. I would think, "I'm the adult here, and I'm supposed to be calm. Why am I joining him?" I prayed and prayed during this time that God would help me to be what Isaiah needed. I wanted God to change me, so no matter how upset Isaiah was with me, I wouldn't get upset too. I wanted God to help me help Isaiah.

I was praying one morning and I cried out to God and felt him saying, "You will never be enough, but I am." I was so scared for Isaiah because it wasn't a good idea for him to go home to mom in the situation she was in at the time. Yet, I was scared I wasn't enough for him either. I was scared I would fail him, and everyone else, if I kept trying to do all the things he needed, and all the things the bigger three needed. I was carrying such a heavy load. It felt like the whole burden was mine. Everyone's future depended on whether or not I could do a good job for them on any given day.

Some days I felt like I would get a passing grade, some days I couldn't imagine a life any better than the one I was living. But other days I was short with everyone, and when Isaiah would scream at me I found myself thinking, "I can't do this much longer." I wanted so badly for God to clearly tell me what to do. He says his yoke is light.[21] This wasn't light. I wanted to hear that Isaiah's mom was doing well, and that there was a healthy future ahead for this little boy with her. Instead, unsupervised visits went back to supervised, and the social worker wouldn't tell me why. Court came and went, without any light in the distance as an answer.

My support worker (a social worker meant to support the foster parent) suggested I get daycare for him; that way I could do homeschooling more easily. I looked into the daycare that was DHR approved near me, and I drove away knowing that was not going to be the answer. I wanted to give him the best, and that answer was not what I felt was in his best interest. I prayed that if there was a better parent for Isaiah that God would please show them to us, but if I was it, then I would gratefully accept. I knew God formed Isaiah and breathed life into him. I believed there was a good purpose and plan for his life. I just didn't know if I was the one to walk with him, point him to God, and get him all the help he needed to be the best he could be. How could I be, when I already felt so overwhelmed day-to-day?

Moses

The story of Moses is a good one to call upon in the day-to-day work of fostering. It says in Exodus 33:12-17 that Moses was crying out to God about being in the wilderness with all these people. He was reminding God that this was God's plan, not his plan. He basically says, "You called me out here. These are *your* people. *Your* responsibility."

This is so relatable. You called us all out here. Now what? The Lord answered, saying, "You are special to me." It wasn't just about all the people God called out of Egypt. It was also about

Moses. Moses was special to God, that's why God called him to such a big task. God knows you. He knows your shortcomings like he knows mine. He says we are special to him. Not just the kids he calls us to. That's important to remember. They matter, *and* we matter. He works all things together for all our good. This life is a blessing and not a curse. There is nothing to fear, because God, the creator of the universe, responds to all our questioning with, "I will be with you."[22] If we will only listen closely, and go where he goes, we will be on the adventure of a lifetime. He will be with us, in the valleys and on the mountain tops.

On the Edge of the Cliff

We didn't know it, but our situation was actually turning into more of a cliff, I was close to falling at any moment. We were in the midst of building a house on the land that we closed on, on the day of our first placement. What we didn't know was that the builder wasn't using our money to build our house. Liens started showing up. Calls started coming in. It seemed like all the ways we were trying to be responsible were for naught. We had saved up, we had planned, we had prayed, and now our money was stolen. I didn't realize how much it was affecting me until one day a lady shook her head at me for the way I backed out of a parking spot. The anger that arose in me toward that innocent lady was unhealthy. I wanted to stomp circles on her car. At that moment I just wanted to let it all out. I didn't though. I had told the kids I would take them for a banana split so I did just that. Well, when the ice cream ran out Isaiah went into a screaming rage. I had to put him on my hip, clean up the mess left by the ice cream eaters, and try to ignore that my blood pressure felt sky high. I overheard Kylen tell Isaiah, "You're my favorite baby," on that same day. I questioned how that statement could be true with all the screaming he had been doing lately. She said,

"Doesn't mean he can't be my favorite." She looked at me like I was a nut job. I felt like one, so I figured it was a good look to give me.

Have you ever looked around, and it seems like everyone has it together and they think you do too, but on the inside, you know that you are a big, tangled up mess? That's where I was living. My kids, my husband, they were all loving life, loving our baby, loving me, and I was saying, "I quit!" I knew that I couldn't be what they all needed me to be anymore. I was one headshake-in-the-wrong-direction away from wanting to stomp on cars.

I had always thought and believed Isaiah would either be ours, or he would go back to his mom. Neither of those seemed to be the option. Surely, God wouldn't ask me to just quit on him, right? How do you quit on a baby? Wouldn't I be failing him? Was I already failing him? I didn't want to send him away. Why would God ask that of us? Despite it all, it seemed like God was literally asking me to trust him with Isaiah's future. To let go of Isaiah and let God do his thing. No control. No influence. Do we really believe he is a good God? Or do we believe he needs us to orchestrate his plans for him?

I started trying to be one step ahead of God. What could he need me to do? I looked for options on a Facebook foster family group. No luck. I told the social worker to be looking, but also didn't want her to feel pressured to throw him into just any home, so I didn't give her a timeline. She would come visit and a week turned into weeks, another court date came and went, and she hadn't found anything for him. At the court date, the social worker showed little interest in finding Isaiah a home. She said her best would be to take him for a night. He slept at night. That was not helpful. I was just barely making it day-to-day. I added pictures to a photo album I'd send with him when he moved to his new home. I threw him a one-year-old birthday party so we could celebrate the milestone he was soon to hit.

One morning, before Eric went to work, Isaiah went into another rage. I sat him down on the nursery floor and walked to the kitchen. My husband heard his crying and screaming and went to get him to bring him to me. At that moment I knew I was done. I felt as though someone was about to get put through a wall. Me or him. I told Eric I wasn't safe anymore. I couldn't parent Isaiah any longer, and I was so sorry. I'd tried. I'd prayed. I knew everyone was all fine, but I was not. I told Eric that Isaiah couldn't stay.

I knew I was on the edge of a cliff, and it was about to give way. I didn't want the whole family going down with me. I couldn't hang on any longer and I had to ask Eric to take him to DHR since the social worker wouldn't come. I had to admit that I was done. There were no more options to be checked out. I had to admit that I couldn't do it all. I had to ask Eric to let me let go of Isaiah. It was terrible, but there was no safety for anyone if I continued one more step.

Pride

I believe many of the failures of the system are related to human pride and the desire to be self-sufficient. It's so scary to say I can't do it. I was married, had housing, a loving family, a support system, and a steady paycheck. I felt that I wasn't allowed to have a limit. I felt like the parents, children, and babies that didn't have all I had were the ones allowed to lose it, and be given grace. I wasn't giving myself grace at all. Do you give yourself grace? Do you extend to yourself the same love and forgiveness you give to others?

I wish I hadn't gotten as close to the edge as I did. I wish I had seen all the signs of stress and overload–all the signs that said the end was near. I didn't. But God allowed me to live through it and warn you.

Read the signs. If what was light has gotten heavy, if what was fun is now a burden, if you've exhausted every option for help, if you are losing your cool with everyone around you, if you feel like you're one headshake away from stomping on the hoods of strangers' cars or slamming your head into a wall—you've gone too far. Your good God calls you special, chosen, loved, set apart, and he says his load is light. You can put it all down. You can place a child back into his hands. He won't leave them, and he won't leave you. You aren't a failure. You didn't mess up and say yes to the wrong kid. You said yes, you did everything you could, and then you have to trust God to take it from there. You aren't supposed to walk the whole road with every child. You have to be obedient in the no just as much as you were in the yes.

CHAPTER FOURTEEN

Am I Lost? Will I Make it Out of Here Alive?

BY SHARING THIS PART OF MY STORY, I hope that if you find yourself in a similar situation, you won't give up. I hope to give you the comfort of knowing people have gone ahead of you and were able to move through, so you will be able to, too. I also would like to say there were many of us that experienced the loss of Isaiah, and I've recorded only my experience. It doesn't mean it was also theirs, or that it will be yours. We all handle loss and grief differently. I've shared my experience. I want to share what happened, and what I did to get through, to hopefully prevent you from ever arriving where I ended up. If you have already arrived at a similar place of loss, then I will share what helped me, along with other resources, at the end of this book. All that being said, shall we get back on the road now?

The Grief is Real

Until that point in my life, I had only lost a grandparent that I truly loved and cared about. I was pregnant with my first baby when that occurred. I cried tons, slept tons, and reflected on memories with my now missing Gram. Then, I named my baby girl after the person she would never meet. I did grief well.

I didn't know that you could grieve *immensely* when you say goodbye to a child who hasn't died, and is only moving on in their journey through life. I wish I had known what I experienced was normal. Instead, I found myself thinking God was done with me, and that I shouldn't even be here. I felt I had failed God, Isaiah, and everyone around me.

The first time I thought the world would be better off without me, I was sitting on the back of a parked four-wheeler in the dark. I had just yelled at my sister and ran from the house. I had come to my mom's hoping for rest. When I got there, something small, a hungry neighborhood dog, set me off. My sister wanted me to care about the dog. I was carrying so much inside that I could not carry any other weight, even that of a pitiful looking dog. I don't know what I yelled, but I had to escape. While sitting out there in the dark, thinking my family was inside wondering what got into me, I began to believe that if I wasn't here at all they would all be better off.

I didn't share these thoughts with any of them that night. I just held that thought inside. My husband and my dad told me they could see I was extremely stressed and they combatted the idea that I was crazy, which is what I was declaring to them. They didn't know my thoughts, so they couldn't understand why I felt like I must be crazy. I thought only mentally unstable people wanted to die, so I must be mentally unstable, right?

How did I get to this place? This is not what I signed up to do when I signed up to be a foster parent. I also didn't sign up to make my family hurt because of me. I wanted to help, not hurt. Surely this wasn't God. Surely it was me being a failure.

I didn't tell anyone about any of this. I couldn't speak it. I wouldn't even write it in my private journal. I didn't want any of it to be true, so the only things I would write were the things I wanted to believe. I wrote down the scriptures or songs that had given me hope that day. I did not write that behind my sunglasses I had been crying while pushing kids on the swings at the park. I didn't write that while planting flowers, I made myself quit and leave with my family to get food because I was afraid if I was left alone I might make good on what was repeating in my head: The world will be better off without you. Suicide.

I remember it clearly. Every Sunday I sat in church, wondering when I would quit hearing "suicide" daily. I heard that word over and over in my head. I wouldn't act on it because I didn't want my husband and kids to think it was their fault. I wanted to write them a note and tell them that, but I didn't want the sadness I was living in to be passed on to them when I was gone. It was so painful. I didn't want to live in my pain, but I didn't want to cause them pain either. I wanted to be pulled out of the darkness. But it didn't seem that anyone could help me, especially when I was unable to speak about it to let them in.

I sent a video message to my sisters in a tone that emphasized how much I loved them, but quickly deleted it because it sounded like a suicide letter, which really was what I was thinking. I wanted to be taken from my pain, but I wanted them all to know they were amazing and that I loved them so much, and none of it had to do with them. I was crying. Then I deleted it before they could watch it. I was afraid if the video was sent, or the letter was written, then somehow that made my sad beliefs true and I would be gone. I was trying so hard to just hold on. I wanted so much to believe that God wouldn't let my life end like this. I loved God during all of this time, but I just couldn't understand the road I was on and why it had to hurt so much.

Eventually, going to church and being encouraged wasn't enough. My personal prayers and devotions weren't enough either. Worship music wasn't enough. I didn't quit all those things and declare myself lost. I decided I had to talk and just see what happened. Despite time having passed, and my faith still being strong in who God is, I didn't trust myself to make a good decision. That was scary. I found I was scared of myself. One morning I told Eric that if he left, I wasn't sure I would survive the day. I'm not sure what he said. I know I asked him to change the lock on our gun safe so I wouldn't be able to access anything in a moment of weakness, and he started battling for me in prayer. If I woke up and the anxiousness, hopelessness, and fear was on me, I would tell Eric, "I need you to pray for me, and I need it out loud." That's when the tide started changing.

I still heard the liar's voice, but I was also hearing the truth my husband was speaking over me. I wasn't feeling all alone in the battle anymore. If you don't share what feels like your weakness, and your failure, with someone who loves you and can speak truth over you, you're in a dangerous place.

It was normal that I would feel like life wasn't worth living because I had lost a child I loved with all my heart. The way it ended made it worse because I chose that ending. According to the Mayo Clinic, one of the top risk factors for depression is the loss of a loved one, and listed right alongside it is financial problems. I laughed out loud when I saw that. I was experiencing two big risk factors, and gave myself *no* grace for the feelings I had. At the time of my loss experience, I had no idea my feelings were signs of depression, or that I had experienced things that put me at risk. Despite the not knowing what I was going through at the time, I did do a few things right. I stayed in community. I actually sought community out by meeting friends at the park. I went to church with my family. I kept clinging to my faith, despite doubting it because of my feelings. However, I wasn't telling anyone the whole truth, and I wasn't reading about grief or depression. If I had, I wouldn't have felt so alone and so lost. I would have known these were normal feelings to be worked through after loss. I'm so glad that by God's grace I finally reached a point where I did talk to Eric and that I asked him to help me.

Now I see what I did actually took strength, faith, and courage. I saw none of that for years following Isaiah's leaving. Now, I am proud that I was able to admit that I couldn't meet Isaiah's needs, and allowed him to move to a place that I'm hopeful God had prepared just for him. A place where the mom was capable and called to parent, and could meet the needs of "my" little Isaiah.

I wrote this a couple of years after Isaiah left us, on the anniversary date of when he first entered our home.

Time has allowed me to look at your pictures and not feel pain. Time has allowed me to see God's hand in your leaving.

Thankfully, he keeps giving me glimpses that say "I was in it. He is okay. You're okay. I've got this."

We loved you fiercely.

I grieved you leaving with anger, sadness, and guilt.

But now, I see God's hand was in it. I was supposed to let go.

I wonder what your story is now. I wonder if I'll get to see what you look like one day. The only face I hold is weeks and months old. Now, it is years old! Years have passed. It's hard to believe and yet it feels like the loss was a lifetime ago. It feels like the grief lasted too long. I didn't know that you don't get over grief, you just get through.

Time is strange. It moves slow and fast. It helps and it hurts. Memories of pain fade, but that makes me feel guilty. I should carry that sharp pain forever, shouldn't I? If I don't, is my love less? I think not. I think God is healing my broken heart. He knows I still love you, but he's given you another mother. That mother is to carry your burdens and feel the pain of your hurts.

Goodbye love. I'll never forget you. You taught me so much. I'm sorry I didn't think of you on your birthday, but I know your mom did. That's just not me anymore.

Don't Wait to Talk with Someone

I should have spoken to someone sooner. If not my husband, a spiritual-based counselor, a close Christian friend, or a pastor. I needed someone speaking truth into, and over, me. I also needed someone making me aware that these emotions that were making me feel so crazy were not so abnormal after all. It would have helped, I'm sure. However, I am here to tell you, when you feel crazy, which has been explained to me as when your outside world doesn't match up with your inside world, *talk to someone.* Not just anyone, but someone who loves you, or has been trauma trained and is being paid to help you become a healthier version of yourself.

I'm grateful that God brought me through, despite my less than stellar choices of denial and keeping it all to myself.

Now, I look at the pictures of my time with that little boy with a separation where I can't feel the joy of what it felt like to hold him anymore, but I also can't feel that sharp pain I felt when he left. I would say I don't feel anything but a question mark. I'm waiting for God to reveal to me the joy in knowing Isaiah again, and even the pain of what may have occurred after he left. I want to feel again what it was to love him, but at this time I see hard lessons learned, and the question mark of how the story ends for him and for me. I choose to believe that we haven't ended forever. I'll be looking for him until I leave this world. I pray that I see him in eternity, if not before. Loving him was real and losing him was even more so. However, I would do it all again, for him and for the person I became after surviving in his absence.

I was an energetic, faith-filled, hadn't-been-broken-too-much-yet momma when we met and I fell in love. In his absence I am a healed, faith-filled, been-broken-big-time momma, but in it I found and experienced God's miracle-working healing power. I'm a stronger person now, thanks to him. I am wiser. I am more confident of God's goodness in the pitch-black darkness, and I am more unshakable when things go wrong. I am braver to face scary things because I know that when I cry for help, God is always there.

You should know that God, in his goodness, doesn't always call you to the whole path even though you thought he would. Instead, see how he is allowing you to love and impact more by sometimes only allowing you to play a part of the journey with a child. He asks you to be faithful and to trust him in letting go. Then in time, he can hand you your next assignment.

You have to be obedient in the no, just as you were obedient in the yes. Both take bravery and strength. One makes sense–of course he would call us to a child–but the no doesn't always make sense. His ways are higher than our ways.[23] Always.

Hebrews 12:1-Let us run the race "marked out for us."

When runners race, they don't just run circles around the globe until they fall over. They run a set course, with a beginning and an ending. We have to do the same in the lives of those God puts in front of us. I fully believe, and have found it to be true in our family, that although I can almost always picture loving each child forever and ever as my own, God doesn't mark that out to be my race in most cases. He gives me a start date and I am faithful in showing up to the line. Then I run as hard as I can for the amount of time he has set for me in advance. Often there is an end date or finish line that I'm unaware of when I stand at the starting line.

When I was unsure about my then foster son, I begged God to make me sure, because every other time he had made it clear that I was to let go or hold on. But in this case, it felt like weight kept piling on and God was silent. I believe he needed me to see that I knew the answer was "let go," but I wouldn't have it. Thus, the yoke was not light like God promises. I wasn't experiencing the promised new mercies every morning.[24] Instead, I was inwardly wasting away. Until I could no longer wait for his answer.

I had to let go, and know that if I was to hold on, God would have already shown that to me in all the places I was searching for him. Every option I looked into to help us stay the course with Isaiah had been a clear "no, this isn't it." God never let me in on the "it."

Faith. Bravery. Courage. Belief. I had to choose them to say goodbye. I'll never be the same, thankfully. I'm thankful for what and who God created in me over that span of time. It couldn't have been created in me any other way. I see that *now*.

If you need to say goodbye to a child, and it's not court ordered, you have to ask for them to be moved. I want you to know you are strong, you are loved, you are chosen, and this is not a sign of your weakness or failure. You said yes when many look away. You loved and gave everything to that child. God has a plan for them and for you. Let go, and see it through. God is the Savior of the world, not you. That's a very good thing. The pressure is on him to work this all out for his glory. Let him do it. Let go, live with open hands saying yes to all he guides you to say yes to, and letting go or saying no when he isn't saying hold on or welcome in.

CHAPTER FIFTEEN

*Rocky Mountains to Climb: Out of Breath,
It's Harder Than I Thought*

IN ANY RELATIONSHIP there will be parts of maintaining it that are harder than you expect. Sibling relationships are messy with jealousy, insecurity, and feelings of unfairness being common. The same can be said of friendships and marriages. The relationships you gain as a foster parent will be no different. There will be plenty of elements that are truly hard work.

When I was first married, I didn't have the "Oh, this is so wonderful. I'm so glad I did this" experience. I had more of a "What was I thinking? Who *is* this guy? Wow. So how are we going to make this work for a lifetime?" type of experience.

Y'all ever signed up for something and been in immediate regret? A gym membership you know you aren't going to use. A magazine subscription that is way more work to get canceled than it was to start up. A house, a car, terrible fast-food choices–the options are endless. All those big and little decisions we make and then second guess–they weren't all bad choices, were they?

What about that time I let my daughter have two kittens, even though just looking at a cat will make me start sneezing? Yep, huge regret. For months. I still sneeze as I blow all the cat hair out of the garage on a weekly, if not daily, basis. But it was never about the cats. It was always about the little girl.

It was never about the guy I married as much as it was about me learning to love someone else more than, or at least as much as, I loved myself. Putting someone else's needs above my own. Whew. That's a tough pill to swallow.

Hard Things You Don't See Coming

It is hard to watch a mom get frustrated and short with the baby you love and care for. It's hard to think that she could be the best option for that child. It's hard to avoid thinking that you might be able to parent him or her more effectively. But, can you? You'll never be the person that gave birth to him. You'll never be able to say "You like pickles just like your dad" because you may not even know the child's biological dad likes pickles. Your child may need to be with the person that gave him or her life more than they need your more adjusted parenting techniques. They may need to know, more than they needed you and your husband to swoop in and "save" them, that even if it wasn't easy growing up with a single parent, at least that parent gave all they had. You'll never be enough. You'll never have all the answers that a child needs. You're never, ever the savior.

You can, however, give a child all you have for as long as you can. You can love without holding back. You can encourage the people that they come with to see the good that came from them. Even if you don't see how all of this is "for their best," you can trust in God and know you have done your best and that's all you can do.

I once watched a mom restrict the amount of food her young child could have because "that'll make her [poop] more." Which meant she would have had to buy more diapers she couldn't afford. Going into foster parenting, I didn't know I'd have to witness and let go of a situation like that. I knew that there were children living on way less food than I knew that child had. I understood that I didn't know what it was like to be unable to afford the items that I consider basic needs. I also knew that this mom loved her child. I knew that, for the most part, she seemed to take good care of her. I also realized that I would never be able to say that "this child is my twin" the way her momma could. I told myself that what was going to matter to that child might be the exact things I couldn't give.

I still pray that God provides for that little girl's every need and that she comes to know him as her personal savior. I pray that for her, and I pray that for her mom. I don't know what it would have done to her mom if she had lost her child for good. I'm going to bet it would have done a lot to convince that mom that she was a failure. She wanted to give her baby more than she had been given. That mom wanted to prove she was able to be the mom people were saying she couldn't be. Taking her baby would have left her and her hard work in the dust with empty arms. There's just always so much more at stake than a few extra snacks and diapers.

We Are Not Superheroes

It's really hard to learn that you aren't a superwoman. I never dreamed I'd have to tell a child that they couldn't come to live with me because I didn't have enough of me to meet their needs. A child can't understand that. They see a house that seems to have all the things they want: siblings, toys, food, and loving parents. How could one more child be that tall of an order? Especially when you appear to have more than you need.

Well, I don't have more eyes. I still just have the two I was born with. I can't see everything that every child wants to show me. Although I may want to, it's impossible to give all of them all of my attention, always. I also don't have enough patience. When I take a child on full time, I want to be able to give that child the best version of me that I can. If I was to say, "Well, it's the right thing to do. She wants to live here. We have a bed. We have enough of pretty much anything she could want, but there's not enough of me," then the answer still has to be no.

You don't want to wake up and feel like a failure every day because you signed up out of guilt, shame, duty, etc. You need to know, before you say yes, that God called you to the child that you are saying yes to. It's not you trying to be the hero. Because once you are in the day-to-day, you will fall short and your superhero cape will quickly be torn to shreds. But if God called you to care for this child, you can rest in the fact that your God does not abandon you. He equips those he calls, and there is grace and mercy for you, as well as for the children that you are pouring yourself out for.

But also, just because something is hard doesn't mean you're getting a sign that it's time to quit. Sometimes it just means you aren't in the shape you thought you were. Have you ever jumped into a kickball game with the kids only to realize that kickballs gained approximately ten pounds since your childhood, and now your leg is sore after one swing at the big ole bouncy ball? Same here.

Sometimes you're just going to have to work harder. When there are resources you haven't reached out for, now is the time to reach out. When there is offered help you haven't said yes to, now is the time to say yes. It's hard to admit when you have tried everything you know and you're still not feeling successful. Sometimes the admission that you don't have the answer will allow people to enter your life with tools to make you and your child successful. I know the fears, "They will tell me this behavior or struggle is all my fault, so I might as well not go. They won't understand. How could they? No one does." Silencing the fears is some of the harder work I've had to do, it may be the same for you. I've found on the other side of the fear, there is relief, there is compassion, there is a person who can help and does understand your situation. Go find them.

I feel like I'm in constant training for a better version of myself. Anytime I make ground with one child, another one shows me another area I need to improve. There are days that it's not even 8 a.m. and I'm tired of working. Yet, I make it through somehow, some way (a.k.a. supernatural provision from the heavenly Father). So will you. All days are not created equal. Don't think the rest of your life is going to look like the moment you are lost in right now.

ER Moments

I was given some great advice that helps me avoid getting lost in the hard stuff all the time: see this moment as an ER moment. Yeah, your child(ren) requires a lot of specialized attention. Yeah, it's taking everything in you, but hospitals don't let people live in the ER and neither will you. You'll find the trained help you or your child needs to get the healing they need. There may be parenting classes you need for this specific child. There may be counseling for one or all. There may be medical needs that have to be addressed, or medications prescribed. I don't know. But you will. You will fight for them. You will fight for you. You will come up with a plan. (Ask God to unfold it. He has done it for us *every time.*) You will move out of the ER. Over time you may even be sent to outpatient. This moment is not a precursor for your, or their, entire life. Don't think about the future and what it may hold based on this moment. You cannot cope with something that has not happened and may not ever happen. You can work yourself into a frenzy and get nowhere though. That's super useful…not!

Mountain tops are beautiful but you will certainly get out of breath, and you may roll an ankle trying to get there. That's okay. It's all part of the journey. This climb will prepare you for the next and so on and so on. Pretty soon you may be in the shape of your life and ready for a bigger role that God has for you and that you have yet to even dream of. You won't know if you head back down at the first sign of resistance. Put it in the work. Buy new shoes. Get some extra water. Call a friend to hike with you for the day. Get a coach…whatever you need. You've got this. I'm out here climbing mountains and waiting for you to join me!

CHAPTER SIXTEEN

Road Rash, a.k.a. Self Care

I WAS IN THE ANZA-BOREGO DESERT looking for a metal dinosaur structure. As you may remember, I had tried to drive the rental car at 4 a.m. on a "marked road." See, there are cool metal statues in one section of this desert, along with the amazing early morning stars. I was in pursuit of a dinosaur statue that was farther out than all the rest. However, I found myself afraid that it looked like my rental car got attacked by an angry ex with a very large cactus arm at their disposal. Not good.

After the pre-dawn scare, I decided to go back and walk out, in the daylight, to see the dinosaur. However, I was trying to decide how long that would take me and I wasn't sure I could tell the distance just by looking. I heard someone taking out their trash and thought, "Ask the lady who lives here." Her response was, "I've never walked out there. Been here twenty-five years." I asked her why, thinking maybe there were snakes, or some other wildlife, that kept her from doing so. She responded with, "Exactly. Why?"

Sometimes the locals are not the people to ask, unlike what you might think. If they ever had wonder and awe, they lost it. They have allowed their everyday view to be something they don't even take note of anymore. Don't let their bitterness, complacency, or doubts be your doubts. I've learned that we all have our own version of the story we have lived and although someone may look like they are in the same place as you, they very well may not be. You don't need to curb your excitement because others have lost theirs.

I turned my car around that day and parked at the end of the road. I ditched the sweater and headed out toward the structures. I saw many different types of cacti that I would never see at home in Alabama. I found a geocache and I pretended to fight some metal dinosaurs for pictures to send to my kids. I had one shoe on and one shoe off to hold the phone, which I was using with a timer app. It was a fun and unique experience that was definitely worth the walk. I was sad to think anyone would live there for twenty-five years and never walk out there on a cool fall morning. Not even thirty minutes from where you live, and you ask yourself, "Why would I even go?"

It's easy to get tired, beat down, and blind to the beauty of your surroundings if you don't take care of yourself along the way. If you need a bathroom break, and there's no bathroom in sight, are you able to enjoy the views or are you hyper focused on the exit signs? If you are hungry and every exit has a blank food sign, are you stopping at the possible roadside attractions and enjoying them? No, because when your basic needs aren't met, you are unable to enjoy the ride.

The same is true in the fostering world. You have to rest. You have to let someone else watch the kids sometimes so you and your spouse can go on a date. You have to let someone keep the baby while you take the big kids ice skating. You have to eat breakfast when it feels like there is no time to. You have to make time. You cannot care for others if your oxygen mask never gets put on. I've gone through seasons of keeping quick, grab-and-go smoothie mixes in the freezer, or ready to eat bars stocked at the house, because I knew I would eat or drink those even if I didn't feel like it. You have to stop long enough to ask, "What would help me?" Then take the time to get those things in place, whether it be prepped foods or regular date nights. You have to be okay, or you cannot be what your children are going to need from you.

When we have a newborn and there are nighttime feedings, for a little bit I can run on adrenaline, but eventually my husband will come home in the afternoon and find me face down on the back porch asleep. Truth. He has the picture somewhere, along with another of me face down on the couch around midday. I normally cannot sleep that hard. However, neither you nor I can run at high speed every day, all day. I have had to make a mandatory rest time midday, where the other kids nap, read a book, listen to a book, something quiet and alone so I can sit, sleep, and not be needed for one hour. No, they don't like it. I tell them if you want mom to be in a good mood, this has to be done. I need to not answer questions, or be needed for just a little bit. Once when the kids were twelve, ten, eight, and four, I took my lunch and a really good book to my room. I turned on white noise as loud as possible. I sat and ate my soup and read one chapter in the book I couldn't wait to read more of. I had so much left on my plate for the day, but I knew from experience that I would do better if I gave myself even just a short break. The four-year-old could not survive without knowing where I was, so he knocked three different times. However, I just said, "Hey, I'm eating my lunch. I will be out in just a little bit." I knew from experience if I pretended not to be there and didn't answer at all, he would have panicked and screamed and cried. So, I was kind and quick to reassure him I was coming out soon. I ate my lunch and read one chapter. I bet I wasn't in there alone for fifteen minutes, but the book was *great*! I got my inspirational nugget to think on as I went on with my day, I got the food my body needed, and I only had to answer the same question three times. It takes time to learn about yourself, and thankfully learning about my kids has required me to learn about me too. Growth for all of us, and boy am I grateful.

We have taken a few trips with just the bigger kids. They give so much every single day. They share their mom and dad. They spend emotional energy loving those we choose to say yes to. They spend physical energy hugging, playing, feeding bottles, or taking diapers to the trash. It is rewarding when we acknowledge all of that and give them time without a baby. It fills us all up. This isn't an all-the-time thing, but when we can make it happen, I recognize the value of it and say yes.

Sometimes it's just dad and the big kids going away for a weekend while I keep the baby. Sometimes he keeps the baby and I take the big kids with me to visit my sister and her family. Then other times, a grandparent keeps the baby and we both take the big kids somewhere fun, and do all the things without the interference of nap times and bottles.

It isn't a lack of love for that little one. It is because of all the love we pour out that we see the value in letting ourselves have rest, even for a couple of days. We are all filling our tanks up with more love and energy to pour into that precious soul when we get back. In the meantime, maybe we will make new memories together on a zipline course, and eat dinner at a place where the sweet tea just keeps coming. Laughter, new inside jokes, and new experiences—it's the stuff life is made of, if we allow ourselves the freedom to not be everything to everyone at all times.

I spoke to a lady once who said she had been a foster parent. She appeared to be close in age to me, with young children, and maybe similar paths that led our lives to intersect on that day. Yet, while I was enjoying my foster son and some summertime fun with him, she was telling me of her "PTSD" from some little ones she had. It wasn't encouraging. It wasn't a story with a tip about what she recommended for me so I wouldn't end up like her. It was just a "local who lost their wonder."

What if we took better care of ourselves along the way? If we would rest when we needed rest, talk to someone when we needed to talk, and ask for help when we needed help, could we keep our wonder? Would we then be able to look out on our unique front-yard view and still find the magic in the walk out to the dinosaurs?

Something For You

Have you ever been asked, "When was the last time you did something for you?" I was asked one day when I called a social worker to ask for tips on what to do with my youngest. When she asked me, I couldn't think of anything I had done for me. There was no time for me. No workout. No nap. No reading. Nothing that filled me up could be accomplished because I spent every moment meeting the needs of others and had never considered acknowledging and taking care of my own needs. When she asked me that, and I realized the answer, I wish I could say I made changes. I didn't. I thought she was full of great ideas, but they weren't something I could implement. I had to learn this lesson the hard way.

For one phase of our life, we called in help to clean. At this point I had four children under six years old. One was a newborn with court hearings and parent visits, and I was homeschooling the oldest two. My house being clean is something that keeps me calm. I cannot thrive in a chaotic environment if the chaos is toys on the floor everywhere and papers all over my counter. Multiple kids, schoolwork, and bio-family visits I welcome, but mess sends me over the edge. It doesn't bother me if it's your house. Truly, I'm always wishful that I could thrive in a messier environment. It only bothers me at my house, where I'm supposed to be able to fall asleep without thinking I saw popcorn in, under, and around the recliner. I will have to clean it if I see it, or fight not cleaning it. It's a real problem.

So, in order to be my best for that little baby, we had someone come clean two times a month. Unless you have a personality like mine, you cannot understand the joy I got when I walked into a house with counters and floors cleaner than I could ever make them. It gave me more energy to pour into that little one who needed so much from me. It also gave me the ability to still pour into the three above him who I'd already committed to serving. We didn't hire that service except the one year we cared for that baby. It was something that helped for a season. Don't say no to offered help if it will actually bring you life. Say yes to the things that will fill you, or your kids, up. Let others support you, or give you breaks. When you allow people to help and admit you can't do it all, you can be strengthened and renewed so that, you never become the local who has lost their wonder.

CHAPTER SEVENTEEN

Enjoying the Journey When It's Not What You Thought

When Angel Baby went home, her parent allowed us to keep in contact. We had another child that was never our official placement but is certainly someone we love. When the latter child moved home to home, the foster moms would let us have visits and contact the entire time. It's such a blessing to have continued contact. It's also hard. You want to know how the child is, and at the same time not get on the foster or biological parents' nerves.

The way I handle it is by sending occasional (monthly or less) messages of encouragement to the parent, letting them know I am thinking about them and encouraging them in their role. No requests, just attempts to add value. If I think of a time their child was with us that we still talk about or treasure, I may send a message and tell them that they are still in our conversations, that we are thankful for their lives crossing with ours, and we love praying for them.

When there's a trigger for me, like a holiday, I will reach out and wish them happy holidays and see if there's a way I can support them. We have connections that provide gifts for foster children and families around the holidays. So, if the parent allows it, we may bring gifts for them to give their child, or if they express a need for coats for winter, we may go out shopping and buy coats. We always enjoy being able to serve the families we love. People aren't always open to asking for help. I know that's true of me, so we just try to keep the lines of communication open, always saying we are there for them and we mean that to be true.

You Can't Do It All

Once a birth parent called and asked for help. The mom was in-between housing, without a car, and had two little ones depending on her. She was at a loss as to what her next steps were. She only asked for us to keep the one child we had cared for during their time involved in foster care, and only until mom could get moved to new housing. We were grateful that the mom felt safe and loved enough to call and ask. We dropped our plans for the day, drove a couple of hours to this mom, went to eat lunch, and tried to figure out what was needed and how to help. We have never preferred to hand out money for such situations. We want to be the support that allows the family to figure out how they are going to be the provider for the family. If times are tight and we see that there are additional needs, then yes, we will provide, like with the winter coats we once purchased. But we aren't going to pay the bills and buy the diapers because that's a short-term solution to a long-term need. We have had to say on occasion, "I'm sorry, we aren't sending money or paying for that. Is there another way we can help you?"

Although that answer may be frustrating for a minute, no one has written us out of their lives because of it. We have proven we are there for them, but we aren't the bank they can come to whenever they please. Throwing money at an issue truly is easier. We could feel good and they would be happy, but the next month they would be in the same place. No growth, no problem solving, and what happens when the bank runs out? We must be in it for the long haul. We sometimes have to let the struggle happen and help in tangible, hands-on ways, instead of trying to be the answer.

What You Can Do

Once when we were out of town on a business trip, we stopped to eat dinner, just my husband and me. As we entered the restaurant, I noticed a young lady trying to fill out an employee application while also trying to keep a young baby entertained and calm. I could've said, "Hey, here's some money," and hoped that she knew how to use it for bills, food, diapers and not for less important things. That might have given me a warm, fuzzy feeling, like "Wow, look at me doing so good helping young parents and babies." Or I could've gone to that mom, introduced myself and offered to hold her baby so that she could finish her work application more easily. I did the latter. I enjoyed being able to make that sweet little boy smile. I prayed under my breath for him and his mom to succeed, for God to protect and provide, and be so very close to them.

When the young mother was done, she and I spoke about her son and how precious he was. I introduced her to Eric. We asked if she had eaten dinner, to which she replied that she hadn't. We ordered a meal for her while we waited for ours to come. I left her with my name and number and said, "Let me know if you are ever in our town. We'd love to see you and your son again."

We didn't fix any big issues for her. We just loved on her, loved on her son, and left our number in case one day she is desperate for help and comes across it. Or maybe just as a reminder that someone she doesn't even know said, "Hey, call us. We would love to see you guys again."

That's the kind of beauty you can enjoy if you don't get lost in the depth of all the pain, loss, need, and trauma, or the desire to fix it all for everyone. The redeemer and rescuer is God, and he already sent his son to die for all the brokenness and sin. Now he has gone ahead to prepare a place for us where every tear will be wiped away and every heart made whole in him. God left us here to show his love to others, and point them to him. He did not leave us here to repair what only God and His son Jesus can repair.

God Uses Hard Times

I didn't know that I would love children and have to hand one back to DHR with no idea where he would go. I didn't know I would be asked by a child if they could be my child, and I would have to say, "Not in my home, but always in my heart and life." I didn't know that it would be the way it is, but it's better. It's beautiful. I wouldn't change it. In both of those situations, God set me free to see my true weakness and lack of power. I have little to nothing to offer to change a situation to be what I want it to be, for my good or theirs. Instead, that all rests on God. He does all the true changing. Just as I have learned to give him my hurts and my disappointment, I point the children to him as well.

Long ago, this guy, Jacob, tore his clothes when he learned of his son Joseph's supposed murder. It says in Genesis 37:35 that his family tried to comfort him but he refused to be comforted.[25] He said that he would go down to his grave in mourning.

All the while his son was alive. Yes, Joseph was sold into slavery for twenty pieces of silver. Yes, he would be lied about and put into prison. But the Bible also says that in every bit of that time, "The Lord was with him; he showed him kindness and granted him favor in the eyes of the prison warden."[26] So, while Jacob was back home feeling like he'd mourn this loss for the rest of his life, his son was being faithful to their God and being granted favor. Joseph was walking out a life he didn't ask for and didn't dream of. And I'm sure he couldn't have foreseen how his situation would land him in a palace and in leadership.

We can grieve our goodbyes, or our dislikes of how the story is playing out, but let's know that our God can and is working when we just don't see it. When the brothers that sold Joseph into slavery went to Egypt, they didn't recognize him in his new leadership role.[27] They were a changed bunch though. When Joseph asked them to leave their brother Benjamin with him, they weren't quick to betray a person like they were before. This time, the brothers were willing to give up their own lives in order to let Benjamin go back to their dad.[28] They caused the grief they had witnessed in their dad for all those years. During those years God was working in the brothers to create more loving, more compassionate, and braver men out of them. The picture is always bigger than we imagine it to be.

Genesis 45:5 and 8 say, "And now, do not be distressed and do not be angry with yourselves for selling me here, because it was to save lives that God sent me ahead of you...So then, it was not you who sent me here, but God." I hope my Isaiah can one day say, wherever he might be, "It was not you who sent me here but God." I don't want him to spend his life wondering why the person that cared for him during his first year of life sent him away. I want him to see how God was in that plan all along.

For me, I know that I needed to learn that I wasn't Isaiah's answer, that I wasn't enough, and that I have limits. God allowed me to experience the giving back so I would see that he is the whole answer in all of these children's lives. I needed to put that burden of making all things good for Isaiah back on God, and quit believing that if I didn't or couldn't care for a child for their whole life, that I shouldn't try to at all.

I hope by the end of all of our journeys, pain included, hard decisions not excluded, that we see we were sent by God, and we are still in fact on the path toward the good God has promised us.[29]

Genesis 49:22-26 is Jacob's blessing for Joseph before Jacob passes away.[30] He speaks of how people attacked Joseph, but how he remained steady, and that the steadiness came through the hand of God being upon him. I intend to pray for that same steadfastness to be upon every child that leaves our home. That no matter what they experience on their path, it will be the path to the palace, and they will be held fast by the Mighty God of the universe.

I also pray that over you, my new and brave friends. The path to the promise is never easy. It is wrought with potholes and battles, but you can know in every hard thing that God is with you. As he did for Joseph, God is upholding you. He is protecting you. He is creating in you the exact person he desires you to be. We aren't made into warriors if we never have to fight. We can't be strong and courageous without being put into situations where those qualities are required.

If you want to be filled with faith like the ones who have gone before you, you can know that they weren't just born with an extra dose of faith. That faith was developed because they went through hard times. And *in* those hard times *they chose to believe* their God would show up! When they questioned God, when they doubted him, they kept moving forward, and then he showed up and strengthened that "faith bone." The next time, they trusted him for even more. They kept stepping into places where they would certainly die, drown, or be killed if he didn't show up. They kept calling out to God saying, "Call me out to you. Let me walk on the water with you." Every single time he responded, "Come," and every single time they still had *to choose step* over the side of the boat. They had to step out of their safe place. They had to do that without knowing if they could walk on water. They did it in faith because it was their desire to be like him, and to be with him.

If we want to be like the brave men and women who have gone before us, we will have to take risks. We will have to step out when we are still scared. We will have to believe that even if hard times are ahead, God can and will use them to create in us the qualities we desire.

When God Says, "Come"

As a child, I read about Corrie Ten Boom, a holocaust survivor. Corrie Ten Boom was placed in a concentration camp, while doing what she believed God called her to do. She was arrested for hiding jews from those who sought to kill them. Once placed in a concentration camp, Corrie Ten Boom lived in horrific conditions and experienced the loss of her father, sister, and many others around her. Yet, she didn't lose her faith. Instead, she grew in her faith. She not only kept her belief in God while darkness and evil surrounded her. She shared God with the women placed in her barracks through scripture readings. Once when she was to be stripped down naked to parade in front of the guardsmen, she prayed that God would hide a Bible she was carrying in a small pouch around her neck. God miraculously hid the pouch. God was using Corrie Ten Boom to give others a freedom that would matter in the eternity many were going to face much too quickly. God was with her, and he was always working miracles inside the hard places she was led through.[31]

God will do the same work of miracles in the hard places he leads you through. What is it your heart feels called to? Where do you hear God saying, "Come"? You have to take the first step. You have to give him the chance to create in you the faith and the steadfastness that you likely don't possess yet. However, that's because you haven't gone anywhere yet. You have to get on the palace path. If you can trust him in whatever unexpected things come your way, then you will find his favor will be upon you. He will never forsake you. There will be times you don't see what he is doing, but you must keep reminding yourself of what you believe about your God. Remind yourself of what he does for those who love him, and keep moving forward down that road in faith. Romans 8:28 says, "And we know that in all things God works for the good of those who love him, who have been called according to his purpose." The Bible goes on to say in verse 31, "What, then, shall we say in response to this? If God is for us, who can be against us?" The guards couldn't see the Bible that God was allowing Corrie Ten Boom to use to share the good news of God's love. Neither will God allow anyone to take what you need to bring the good news of his love to the children and families in the foster care system.

None of us are born brave. It's who God creates us to be *as we walk* through hard things, whether by choice or by chance. We all walk through hard things. It's who we are looking for while we are in hard places that is going to make all the difference. If you are looking for him, you'll find him. My favorite verse as a child was Matthew 7:7, which says, "If you seek you shall find; knock and the door will be opened to you." Knock. Seek. He's there. He is waiting for you to knock. He is waiting for you to ask for him and say, "tell me to come to you on the water."[32] If you want to walk on water, get going. You'll do it. He has his hand out saying, "Come."[33]

CHAPTER EIGHTEEN

Please Be Cautious of Desert Wildlife: Boundaries

OKAY, SO IN MY HOUSE ERIC has a cup that he keeps ice water in, every day, all day. All four kids know this, so if a child comes inside and is thirsty, they will reach for dad's cup. The kids know what is in the cup and they know dad doesn't mind them drinking it. On the other hand, I like to drink a carbonated mineral water called Topo Chico, and if the kids see one sitting out, icy cold and ready for consumption, they are usually wise to ask before they touch it. For whatever reason, I can only share if I feel like I have a choice in the matter. If you assume that you can have my drink and take it without asking, it's highly likely there will be some sort of lecture or angry response from me.

Since I don't want to lash out at my kids, this boundary or preference of mine has been addressed from the time they could understand what was being said to them. I set my husband and children up for success by setting a boundary before an infraction occurs.

It's not mean to set boundaries; it's wise. We all have things that keep our family running smoothly. For example, maybe we have to set time slots for guests who tend to stay over too long. By setting the boundary, and letting them know we only have a certain amount of time, it allows us to enjoy their presence without constantly worrying about how we will get them to leave, or worse yet, never inviting them over because we don't want to have to set a boundary.

You must have boundaries for yourself and your family. You must be the one to hold the line because the foster system has more need than it has resources. Social workers may leave you feeling used or taken advantage of. Not necessarily intentionally, but out of their own survival and self-preservation.

If you could pack your whole family up and take a child to a visit, but it means that nap times will be missed, it will be hard to make dinner, or you will be tired because it's a lot of work, you can say, "No, I cannot take the child to the visits. You (the social worker) will have to arrange for transport." Just because you can, does not mean you should. I could go to Chick-fil-A today and drink a whole milkshake, and then do the same tomorrow, and the next day, and the next day. Maybe for a whole month. Maybe I would feel perfectly fine for a few weeks. But at some point, it is all going to catch up to me. I will have put on some pounds that will be way harder to lose than they were to add, and I will wonder, "How did I end up here? What was I thinking? Why did I think all those milkshakes were a good idea?" Perhaps the guilt and shame, and beating myself up, would drive me back to Chick-fil-A for another milkshake.

That's a delicious sounding mistake. However, it's not so funny when the additions are children, or needs of all those around us. Yes, we enjoy meeting the need, but we need to ask ourselves if what it takes from us is more than what's being poured back into us. You can only sustain a life of "pouring out" for a short amount of time. Then you will find yourself bitter or irritated each time someone needs something from you. Maybe the needs are ones you used to love to meet but now you don't. A social worker cannot be expected to recognize your fatigue and come to save you.

Don't let it get to where you want to stomp cars in the parking lot, throw sandwich meat down on the floor and run away from the grocery store, or kick a dog in the butt just for needing to be cared for. If you are feeling like you could hurt the kids your promised to love and protect from being hurt, or worse, then your tank is too empty and it's time to call for a halt. You cannot give what you do not have. It will be best that you trust God with the children and have them placed elsewhere. I don't want it to be you who needs the cops called because you lost your mind. Don't think it's possible? Think you're above losing your mind? Well, you're wrong. I'd rather tell you now so that you can see the warning signs and get yourself and your children the help and safety you and they need.

We don't need any more seemingly-wonderful humans on the news, found to be hiding the evil we thought they were protecting people from. Maybe they just had too many people thinking they were a hero, and they liked the feeling of doing good things, until the point where they ran out of the energy to do the things they once loved and they were too prideful to admit they had reached the bottom of the energy tank. Maybe that's not it. I believe most people want to do good. No one sets out to be a foster parent with the intent of being the scary story we all hear and wish wasn't true. So how does it happen? I think unhealthy boundaries, or lack thereof, could be part of the cause of the crash-and-burn stories and experiences.

Guardrails

When we drive on the road and there are guardrails, do we aim our cars at them? No, we know they are there to protect us from whatever lies beyond that could seriously hurt or kill us. You need those same guardrails here. There's no magic number of children you can have, or criteria that says, "You can meet this many needs with this amount of children." Children are all different, with different needs. You add in trauma and there are higher levels of needs that can be expressed in several different ways. Things I can handle you may be triggered by, and so the children I have could be too much for you, or vice versa.

My family is great with babies, so we have an infant to two-year-old boundary. You may choose fifteen years and up as your boundary. We started our fostering journey only approved for one child. Maybe you are approved for three so you can provide shelter for a sibling set. Each of us decides these boundaries at the beginning of our time as a foster parent, and we adjust as we learn more about ourselves on the foster-parenting road.

Over time, maybe you will find there has been more healing and growth in the children that are already in your home, and at that time you will be equipped to change your boundary lines. I just want you to know they are where they should be right now, and don't let what anyone else seems able to do guilt you into more than your family can take on. With every child you say yes to you, you give your all, and that's your best yes. If my best yes is one tiny baby and yours is a sibling set of three, that's ok. We are different people with different support systems in place, and our children are different children with different needs.

Do not jeopardize the healing of the ones already in your home with your need to keep providing a safe place for the children CPS keeps calling you about. Trust those children to God, and continue to give your all to the ones in your home. When you're able give your best, and feel God urging you to say yes again to the one they call about, then go ahead (if you have the full support of those already in your home).

When it comes to boundaries with biological family and your foster family, those are up to you. Everyone does it differently. For us, I like to go to the preset court dates at all possible opportunities so I get the chance to encounter the biological family and start a relationship. I have a Google voice number that

I share with them so I can get a different alert when they message. With this in place, I'll know who it is that's calling or messaging and answer and respond accordingly. With some parents/guardians we have visits outside of the in-person visits that are court ordered, and with some we have not. That's where I ask the social worker for their suggestion. Sometimes the worker is clear that they don't think it's a good idea, and other times they are quick to say, "Oh yes, I'll give them your number." As time goes on, you will see what works best for you.

Because each child responds differently to visits, sometimes a visit is a trigger and your in-home child will be disrupted with extra visits. Sometimes the visits are needed for their parents' mental health and peace, but you have to be able to say, "No, that won't work for us today, but here's a picture or a video of them." Try to be flexible. Think of what you would want if the roles were reversed. Pray about it before you offer or respond. Sometimes I agree to things that I feel like I've got to do despite not wanting to disrupt the flow at home, and other times I have the feeling I have to say, "No, we can't do that at this time."

The Biological Family

I feel obligated to the biological family. At the same time, I've learned that sometimes the biological family can negatively affect the child in my care, as well as the rest of our family. For example, extra visits for our youngest son Jaxon, would cause him to have night terrors for up to a week following the visit. Nothing had happened to him at the visit. Sometimes we just met up and had waffles with his birth mom. But it still affected him, and in turn it greatly affected us and our week following.

Your first priority is to the child; however, that is his or her birth family. I always want Jaxon to know that I did everything I could to support his first family and let them know I love them.

However, if they were asking for more visits and I knew that meant he would be upset more weeks than he would be settled, then I would say, "We can't do that right now, but hopefully soon."

Of course, you will need to make sure the child is at all court-ordered visits. You will not have a right to refuse. It's the visits outside of the court-ordered visits that will require careful discernment about what's best for the child. With our first placement, the mom wanted FaceTime calls almost every day. That was very disruptive to my day with four children young children, but she was a young mom and I knew she just wanted to see her little one. Sometimes I let the kids hold the phone so she could see her baby as we drove to the pool. Sometimes I let the kids run wild and hoped they weren't in the road while I showed her the baby crawling around.

Looking back, I do wish I had said at the beginning of the call, "Hey, I have 10 minutes, then I'll have to let you go, but here is your sweet baby." Then I wouldn't have been sweating and wondering when and how I could kindly end this call. I had to learn to set expectations and boundaries. Boundaries are good, healthy, and safe. If your heart toward the biological family is one of love at all times, and especially as you decide how to form the boundaries you think are needed for everyone, you will make the right decisions.

When Boundaries Are Crossed

We set boundaries to keep ourselves, and the people we care about, safe. Safety may not mean protection from physical harm, but maybe emotional distress, or protection of your available time. However, I've set boundaries before, like a time limit on a visit, only to have the time limit ignored. When boundary lines are crossed you have the option of packing up and leaving when you said you would leave, or you could choose to have a discussion with the people involved. They may not understand, and if it exhausts you to have to enforce the boundary, then you will sacrifice less time for the family.

I know our friends and family outside of our home love to love on our people, but our young people have experienced hard things. Our children may not feel comfortable with hugs, or even an arm around their shoulder. The adults and older children in our lives can be educated politely without the foster child being present. Outside adults don't need to know the details of a child's history to respect that they will be expected *to ask* for a hug or a high five, and that they will not be allowed to pout or fake sadness to guilt our child into crossing a line they want to stay behind.

I have a close friend who spent the better part of a year, two times a week, an hour at a time, trying to gain the love of my awesome little Jaxon. She and I were doing life together, so Jaxon saw her *often*. However, he was very slow to let her into his circle of trust. She respected that, saying things like, "That's okay," after being turned down for any interaction, "one day we will be friends." Jaxon certainly came around. We knew she was fully in when one morning at a prayer service Jaxon asked to go to her. They did several laps walking and praying, sometimes with her hand on his shoulder. They were officially buddies. No guilt, no bribes, just consistent showing up and respecting his space. That's what it took.

We need to remember we are also modeling how relationships work to our children, whether biological or fostered. Our children need to know they have a voice, and no matter their age, their voice and their feelings matter. Our children need to know they can set physical boundaries, such as not hugging grandpa because it feels uncomfortable, and that boundary will be respected. Our children need to know if the boundary is not respected, then the adult keeping them safe will talk to the adult that crossed the line. There may or may not need to be consequences for boundaries that are crossed. If people have good intentions they most likely will not be offended when you stand up for yourself or your child. The people who get angry and defensive, are the ones who feel caught.

I have found it easy to set and protect boundaries for my children, but harder for myself. I won't sacrifice my child's well-being, but I will possibly sacrifice my sanity by agreeing to do too much for others. However, when I think of how I want my kids to set boundaries and protect themselves as children and adults, I realize that means I'm not only allowed to set and protect my own boundaries, but that I need to practice doing that in front of my kids so they will be equipped to follow suit.

CHAPTER NINETEEN

Starry Night Gazing

WE CALLED HIM LITTLE BROTHER, because he was the little brother for that entire year. Isaiah really loved to sit and watch the wild "big" kids. They would flip and flop and laugh as they fell out of hammocks, and he would sit in the grass smiling. Our new puppy would go and lay beside him. Isaiah would take handfuls of soft, brown, curly puppy fur in his hands, and all was right in the world.

In the mornings they would all line up on the couch to drink cocoa and Kylen would wrap Isaiah in her most prized pink blanket while he drank his bottle of milk. They would all be calm, quiet, and happy. I would take a picture in moments like that and send it to Eric. We felt so blessed. We *were* blessed. He was ours and we were his. His newborn pictures were on the fridge; a big picture of all four of them was on the living room wall.

Those are the moments I try to sink into deeply, almost holding my breath, willing it to last longer. The moments you never want to forget. The first glimpse of a flashing heartbeat on an ultrasound screen. The view of the one you love waiting at the end of the aisle to commit their life to you. A clear, starry night sky with more stars than you ever remember seeing before. Those moments are found on the road to being a foster parent, too.

There for the View

I remember looking through the glass of a tiny room outside of the courtroom where "our" baby son was being held for the first time by his biological dad. His dad talked to him like a person talks to a baby–with smiles and coos. I snapped a picture. I didn't know where the road was leading for either of them, but I knew that this moment was one to hold onto. If I hadn't been there, who would be able to tell my son about his first dad? If you Google him, you won't find what I saw when I watched him hold his baby. You won't read about how he handed him back to me and said, "Thank you for letting me hold him." Thank you. He thanked me for letting him hold *his* son. That's heartbreaking. But I was there. I got to witness what no one else has ever witnessed with these two. That's a once-in-a-lifetime, starry night view. That view is worth more than this world has to offer.

You could be the one to take a child to their first Christmas light show, parade, drive-in movie experience, sunset on the beach, or family dinner where laughs and love abound. You might introduce a child to chalk art on the sidewalk on a cool spring afternoon, or finger painting a pumpkin until there is more paint on the child than the pumpkin. Those moments can't be bought. They can't be faked. They are worth more than gold.

If my only job is to get a little boy off of the table 100 times today, that's okay. If my job is just to tickle him and hear his amazing laugh, then I have the best job in the world. God's job is the mending of hearts, the repairer of all that is broken. I can't do those things, and he didn't ask me to. He just asked me to tell his kids that he loves them and to tell them he will wipe away every tear. God will make something beautiful out of all our messes. He has the hard job. Ours is easy, as long as we don't start thinking we are in charge of his job.

It's not like God forgets who he is, but we sure seem to. He knows what he is capable of and I believe he likes to hear us reminding ourselves of the things he has already done, and the things we know he can still do. We can't think of things bigger and greater than he is capable of. He will always be able to do more than we can imagine. Let's give him a lot of room to show himself to us, and through us, to the watching world, by opening up our lives. Many lives will be changed; you'll be surprised that the biggest and best change will probably be inside of you. You'll learn to trust him more quickly, believe him more readily, hold on to him more tightly, and you'll find yourself in a life of high adventure.

Golden Buzzers

Not only is the adventure going to change your life, the people in your world will also be changed. We have two families that we know on the edges of our lives. They weren't people we saw all the time, or even knew really well, when we talked to them about fostering. Both families spoke to us, asking questions about our foster-family life. Both families went on to become foster families themselves, and both have now also adopted from foster care. This shows me that this story isn't about us, it's about what God can do with us. It's a great honor to play any small part in more children and parents finding each other and becoming family.

Have you ever watched *America's Got Talent*? People from all kinds of backgrounds get the chance to go on stage, and do the things they believe they were made to do. The watching world either agrees or disagrees by voting. There is a limited amount of golden buzzers. Each judge, and the host, gets one. When they see someone they cannot imagine being anywhere but on that stage, they smash a big gold button and the confetti pours down. It's a dreamlike moment. When the golden buzzer is pushed it means that person automatically gets sent to the live rounds with no chance of being cut until the world gets to see them and vote. We love when someone gets the golden buzzer. When someone gets out on stage and does their thing, your arms get chill bumps, and you think, "Wow, that's what they were born to do." That's when we all start chanting, "Golden buzzer, golden buzzer," from our couch. We haven't been wrong too many times because when you were born to do something, the watching world can easily see it.

I love to see the person's face, and their family's faces. You know a lot of hard work has led to that moment, but on that day there's nothing but smiles, cheers, and golden confetti falling. There is something magical about it all. Well, when people watch you get out of the truck, car, or van with a bunch of little kids at the pool, and you walk in smiling, ready to do some can-openers off the board, gold confetti may not rain down, but the world is watching. When you're doing what you were made to do, there's a joy, a fulfillment, that comes with it that is pretty close to magical. I've had some golden buzzer kind of days, and I want you to do the thing that gives you that same golden-buzzer feeling.

Blurred Lines

Once we were at the river on a hot summer Saturday. Our youngest foster love was splashing around in his float, and the older kids were jumping off the rope swing. I'm not sure how the conversation started between myself and a teen boy that was also out there, but I remember it ended with him telling me, "He sure looks like he thinks he is yours." Isn't that the goal? To love someone so well that the line between yours and mine is blurred? That teenage boy was right. Our littlest did believe he was ours, because we loved him as if he was. It didn't matter that there might be a point in the road where he would either walk away with the parents that brought him into the world, or walk away with us. Right then, in that moment, he was ours and we were his, and there was no reason to love him with anything held back.

On any given day you will hear me ask that same little boy, "Who's the best?" He replies with "I am." I don't ask because my other children aren't also the best. I didn't ask because I knew he would one day be a Fillebaum. I taught him that because I want him to succeed, and for him to succeed he needs to believe deep down in his soul that he has much worth, much value, and that no matter what has happened or will happen I, and his Father in heaven, know that he is the absolute best and is capable of big and wonderful things. Hearing him reply, "I am," is another starry-night moment for me. It brings all the noise, and all the hard, to a quiet calm where I can sink into a small moment and know that all is right with this little piece of the world. In fact, I will generally ask him, "Who's the best?" after a hard moment has occurred. I do it to remind us both that this moment is more than what I am currently seeing, and I must press into my soul that this work is worth every bit of the effort required.

SECTION III

End of the Road

CHAPTER TWENTY

Hear from the Kids

ONE OF MY BIGGEST CONCERNS when beginning as a foster parent, while also raising young children in my home, was how it would affect them. Instead of telling you about all the positives I've witnessed in them through the fostering experience, I asked them to speak for themselves. As it says in Psalm 8:2, "Through the praise of children and infants, you have established a stronghold against your enemies, to silence the foe and the avenger."

Jaxon, age 3

He has been a foster brother to five little ones. Most for only a night or a few nights.

> Me: What do you think about us being a foster family to little babies? Do you want more babies to come?
>
> Jaxon: I don't let babies come in my room.
>
> Me: What about _____? Can she go into your room?
>
> Jaxon: (He smiles.) Yes.
>
> Jaxon remembers our last respite placement very fondly. They were cuddly buddies during the week she spent with us. He was quite sad that she wasn't going to stay with us forever. She slept in the room we put together just for our

foster loves and he was in the boys' room. But unlike other babies we've cared for, she was allowed to play in the boys' room with whatever toys he was keeping away from *the babies*.

Holden, age 10

He has been a foster brother to nine little ones. He has been a foster brother for more than half of his life at this point.

Me: Has this experience caused you pain more than it's caused you joy?

Holden: No, no, no. It's a lot more joy than it is sadness. I just think that if you are wanting to start foster care, it is going to be hard and sad, but it's going to be great. You will get to help a lot of babies.

Me: Tell me your favorite fostering memory.

Holden: Showing all the little babies what I like to do. Like when I showed Selah how to break Duplos over her head. I would build a tower and bang it on my head and she would do the same thing. And when Richie was here with Jaxon and they were sitting on the picnic blanket out front playing together. Jaxon was so little. I just like seeing babies having fun together. And they are just cute!

Me: Worst foster care memory?

Holden: Who was it when we were eating candy on the counter?

Me: William.

Holden: I had stopped crying but Kylen had not stopped. It was sad. He [William] was leaving. I didn't want him to leave. That's the one I thought was going to be my brother.

Me: Do you think other people should do this? Would you do this on your own or with your family in the future?

Holden: Yes. I wouldn't do it on my own, but I would do it with my own family. Other people should do this because we need more people to help the babies. There aren't enough people helping.

Me: What makes you say there aren't enough people helping?

Holden: I feel like there are just a lot of babies. Like I told you, I felt like we didn't help enough babies because we couldn't take the baby that needed us that day. I wanted to know that they were going to go somewhere, and not just sitting in an office.

Me: How did that make you feel?

Holden: Sad. Because we have so much here to do and that tiny baby was just sitting in an office with nothing to do and no one loving them.

Me: If you were to tell me what foster care is, what would you say?

Holden: Fostering is where CPS asks you [the foster family] if you can take in a couple babies to help. They need a family to take care of them because their biological family can't take care of them.

Me: So, how long do you keep the babies?

Holden: There really isn't a time limit. Each baby has a different time limit. Sometimes, it's two weeks, sometimes it's one night, and sometimes it's a year. Or in some cases, their whole life.

Me: Do you wish we didn't do this?

Holden: No.

Me: Why?

Holden: Because I love babies. They sit with you. Three-year-olds don't. I would rather hold a baby for a day or two than go to Cash Bro's [a motorcycle riding place he loves] or play Fortnite.

Me: If I told you that you couldn't play video games all month so that we would have the time to take care of a new baby, would you say yes?

Holden: How old is the baby? Do they have any extra needs?

Me: What kind of needs do you mean?

Holden: Like do they have any tubes or extra medicines that would make it harder to take care of them? Like that one baby we went to meet.

Me: No extra medical needs. What do you say? Whatever age you want.

Holden: Day old. No, two days old. The cute kind. I would say yes.

Me: Well, that's pretty cool to hear Holden.
(When I wrote this, video games were an everyday begging obsession. I'm so glad babies ranked higher than that!)

Kylen, age 11

Has been a foster sister to nine little ones.

Me: Best fostering memory?

Ky: Hmmmm. Lots of fun ones. Can it still be Jaxon? Teaching him how to walk was fun just because most of the babies were too little to learn how to walk when we had them. It was exciting because I can remember it and was old enough to remember it.

Me: Worst fostering memory?

Ky: Mmmmm. Which baby was it that we dressed in cute clothes and only had for one day?

Me: William.

Ky: Yes, it was fun seeing him, and dressing him because that's my favorite thing to do. It was sad because we barely had any time with him. He came at nighttime and left without it being a whole day.

Me: Looking back, is there anything you wish you did differently or anything you could recommend to people who may experience this [sad loss] too?

Ky: Try to stay positive. Help others and remember that there are probably going to be more babies you can help, and you have helped others and been sad before and it was still worth it. Have as much fun as you can. Enjoy the moment, take pictures, and don't think about when they are going to leave. I don't think I would change anything, because we did all of that when he was here.

Me: Would you foster when you are older and on your own or have your own family?

Kylen: Probably yes. It depends, because I want to travel around the world, and you can't do that easily while fostering because you have to get permission to take them. I would foster while I'm trying to save money for traveling.

Me: Would you recommend other people to do this?

Ky: Yes, definitely would love for other people to do this. It's fun, and you're helping babies and families.

Me: As the oldest, is there any extra pressure when we add to the family in this way? What makes you okay with it?

Ky: Yes, definitely extra pressure. I already have to help with Jaxon a lot, and I have to help more than the other siblings so there is less chill time when a new baby comes. I'm okay with it because it is helping others. I love helping others because if they can't help themselves, I like to help them because everyone needs help.

Me: How do you respond when people ask, "Who is that?" and they are asking about your sister or brother who is a foster sibling?

Ky: If they ask me if that's my sibling I say, "Yes." If they push further with, "Why don't they look like you?" I say we foster little kids and help them. It's only happened once and the kid didn't really care about my answer and ran off, so I don't know what else I would say.

Me: What about when they ask about ones who are adopted?

Ky: I usually just say, "She or he is adopted." That's it. I do get that a lot.

Me: If you were talking to a mom or dad who is scared that this experience will be too hard on them or their children that are already in the home, what would you say?

Ky: The first one was the hardest. It got easier after the first one. You know what's probably going to happen so it's easier to have fun with them, and know it's probably not going to be forever. You know that you are just helping. Once you hear about their family, and you know they need help, you help them for a period of time knowing that you can't keep everyone forever. There would be too many and it would be a stressful mess.

Me: Truth!

Anne Marie, age 8
Has been a foster sister to nine little ones.

Me: Best fostering memory?

Anne: The first one. Just how cute she was. I think I held her.

Me: Worst?

Anne: I don't have one.

Me: Would you do this when you are older?

Anne: Maybe. Because I like helping and I like seeing cute babies. But I don't like getting up in the middle of the night if they are screaming at me.

Me: Would you recommend this to people considering it? Why?

Anne: Yes, so babies, bigger kids, and their families can get help.

Me: How does it change your experience in the home when someone new comes?

Anne: Fun because they are cute, and when Jaxon holds a baby it's really cute because he gets this really cute smile. It makes me happy because they are cute.

Me: What about when they leave?

Anne: It is sad but I don't cry like y'all.

Me: Why don't you cry?

Anne: (Shrugs shoulders.)

Me: What have I told you about when everyone else is crying and you are cartwheeling by?

Anne: I don't remember.

Me: Were you sad when William left?

Anne: Yes, a little bit.

Me: Did it look like you were sad when you cartwheeled by the crying bigger kids?

Anne: No.

Me: I told you it was okay that you didn't cry. We all deal with sadness differently. I said it would be nice if you just didn't cartwheel right in front of the older two because it made them think you didn't care about his leaving. Or if the cartwheels had to happen, then at least tell them you are sad and you do care, but you just don't cry, you cartwheel. Do you remember any of that?

Anne: No.

Me: Well, does it make sense?

Anne: Yes.

CHAPTER TWENTY-ONE

The First Goodbye

THE DAY ANGEL BABY LEFT US, we knew it was possible that she would be going home. We knew her mom was going to court that day and it could mean that Angel Baby wouldn't need our care any longer. Her mom was going to show them what all she had gotten done during her baby's stay with us. I'm so thankful for the relationship with her mom, for more reasons than one. It was good on this day because as soon as court was over, she called me and told me they had given Angel Baby back to her. Who knows when the social worker would have gotten around to letting me know. (They have way too many things to keep track of.) Mom asked if I could bring her to them. I couldn't. It was decided that since the social worker that was working the case had to take the mom to get a car seat and other things they wanted her to have, they would stop and pick Angel Baby up at that time.

I had already prepped Angel Baby's things, just in case, but now her departure was real. I gathered her new duffle bag with her nicknames written all over it in Sharpie. I gathered all the baby food. I took a picture of her and all her things on my kitchen floor. The kids and I went out to our back porch to hang out together before she left. I still look at the picture we took of all of us on the couch together smiling with "our" Angel Baby. I baked cookies to send with mom for the ride back home. I tried to comfort the kids saying how happy her mom was going to be and that it would be cool to meet her, in person.

An hour or more later, the social worker pulled up. She was frazzled and hurried, and mom wasn't with her. I asked where she was and she informed me she had left her at a nearby store while she came to pick up Angel Baby. We were not happy about this unexpected change in plans. We wouldn't meet mom and I had to strap Angel Baby into a car seat with a stranger driving. I brushed the snacks, left by a previous child, out of the seat and placed our little love in a car seat that wasn't even her size. This was not at all how I had pictured this first goodbye. I did what I had to do and the lady left quickly.

I turned to the kids, and of course the older two were crying. I could hardly look at their faces. They were sobbing! I pushed us all back into the house and I called my husband saying the only words I could choke out: "She's gone."

The big kids were saying Angel Baby's name over and over through their sobs. I asked them, through my own tears, "Well, now that we know what this feels like, would we do it again or just say no?" They said, "Do it again but *only* for Angel Baby." I felt the same way. My oldest daughter, Kylen, was gasping as she cried, "I love her too much."

I declared to everyone, "Get in the truck. We are going to have Yogurt Mountain for lunch." We all tried to wipe our faces and look forward to an untraditional lunch plan to calm us down. As I went to get socks for the kids, Holden came to tell me that Kylen was outside crying about how I couldn't make them stop crying, to which Holden added, "She was too cute!"

My husband pulled up as we were buckling in. He got out of the car and we could see he was upset too. That set us all off again. The big two ran to him and he picked them both up. They were hugging his neck with arms tight around him and sobbing into his shoulders. We told him our lunch plan and he agreed to join us before heading back to work.

We made our way to Yogurt Mountain and when we parked, I got out and told Kylen and Holden to stand beside the truck while I went to get Angel Baby. I opened the truck door and my little Anne Marie looked at me and said, "I not Angel Baby."

All of that to say, the goodbyes are hard, and the pain is real. It has been helpful for me to focus on comforting the children already in my home, because I've heard myself telling them how God cares about them, and he cares that they are hurting. When the child you loved is gone, it can be easy to think that if God cared about you, he wouldn't let you feel the pain of a goodbye. He will let you feel pain, he will let you experience heartbreak, but he doesn't ever leave you there. He is in the hard places with us. He longs to comfort us and bring healing. He never leaves us or forsakes us.[34] When I kneel to remind my crying children of the truth of God's love and care for us, and not just the one who left, it's as if God is whispering to my heart, "I care about you too, and I'm sorry that you hurt."

The evening that Angel Baby left, I took the kids out to watch the sunset while waiting for Eric to get home from work. I thought to myself, "Well, we have made it through the first day. That's something to be proud of. We have now done something we all thought we couldn't do."

The next morning her mom sent us two pictures and a video of Angel Baby. She was so kind to keep us in the loop. She followed through with her promise to keep us in their lives. I saw with this first goodbye that God was good, and I chose to continue to trust his plan.

If I had written Angel Baby's story, I might be the only one who benefitted—or at least the person who benefitted the most. But he wrote a story that benefits way more than me. I am determined to trust in him. I have many scriptures underlined in my Bible with a baby's name next to it, or a date and note written off to the side. That's how I remind myself what God has promised for those he created and those he loves.

I have Psalm 9:10 underlined in my Bible, reminding me that those who know God's name will trust in him. If you have to hand a perfect angel back to her mom, then you must also trust that God is going with her. If you were obedient in taking her in, then you need to be obedient in trusting him when she goes home. The verse goes on to say, "For you, Lord, have never forsaken those who seek you." You may feel the need to remind God you are doing this for him and his babies; therefore, you are also trusting that he isn't calling you here only to be broken-hearted forever.

One morning, before we started the fostering classes, I woke up early because I heard someone saying my name. I found that Eric was not in our room, and no one else was awake, so I replied like Samuel in the Bible: "Speak God, I'm listening."[35] This is the only time in my life I audibly heard God's voice. I heard him tell me, "This will be fun." So, when I had to say goodbye to Angel Baby I reminded God that he had said, "This will be fun," and saying goodbye was not fun! I wasn't calling him a liar, but I wanted him to know I was still counting on *more fun*. No one will deny that knowing Angel Baby and loving Angel Baby was fun.

After the goodbyes, you must be determined to keep walking forward with God. He will continue piece by piece, step by step, to give you a view wider than you, your family, or your sadness can see, as he asks you to hand each little one back to him.

Sometimes Your Role is Just to Love

Only a week later, we got a call about a three-day-old baby girl. We were either going to be busy or out of town for the next three weekends. I said no. I told the lady who called we had just finished a short-term placement and were only interested in forever. She said they weren't going to be able to tell me that on any call. She said even if five siblings have been adopted before, the sixth one is a new case. CPS will have to treat it as its own case. CPS must explore every bio-family option first.

I told the kids about the call and how CPS wouldn't be able to tell us if it's an adoption situation up front. I told them we would have to choose to risk experiencing the Angel Baby goodbye again. Both big kids agreed it was a no unless it was Angel Baby. I said, "Okay, well it's not. It's a tiny baby girl. I will keep asking you when they call." Kylen said, "Okay, well this one is a no." And so, it was.

It had been a few weeks since Angel Baby went home. We had a free weekend so I asked Angel Baby's mom if we could come visit. She agreed. We didn't tell the kids just in case mom canceled at the last minute. We didn't know her that well. We told the kids that we were exploring a new part of town. We took some desserts with us because Angel Baby's mom just had a birthday. When Kylen saw who we were meeting she smiled ear to ear and said, "Oh my goodness, oh my goodness!" It was great! I enjoyed hugging and kissing little Angel Baby. We all enjoyed spending time at a park playing and eating together. I cried on the drive home.

Driving away was so hard. I learned more about Angel Baby's mom and how she had experienced foster care herself. How she wanted better for her child. I just wanted to fix it all. Angel Baby's mom felt like my kid too. I couldn't help but imagine

Angel Baby's mom was just Angel Baby in an older body. It felt like too much, to care so much about both of them and have to drive away. Again, I tried to remind myself that our God is a big God. I also thought maybe this feeling of weight, or continued burden, is why people don't try to be involved with biological families. I will admit, it's so hard to watch and wait and have no control over what's going on with those you love. Would it maybe be easier if we didn't know? We decided that the burden of knowing was worth bearing if it meant we still got to see Angel Baby and her mom.

In the next month we had Angel Baby and her mom come stay with us for a weekend. It was so great to have Angel Baby back in our house. We spent the weekend doing family things. We all went and watched Holden in BMX races. We played at our local science center and went to church on Sunday morning. I loved taking pictures and got tons of mom and Angel Baby, as well as all of us and Angel Baby. I looked over on Sunday and Eric was holding Angel Baby during worship. I saw the love of a dad for his daughter on his face. Again, I thought, "Why can't she just stay? We love her so much." Mom asked for her baby girl back and Angel Baby fell asleep on her mom's lap. We both loved this baby girl, but it was her baby. I tried to come to terms with my role. My role was not to parent. My role was, apparently, just to love.

My mom and I were the ones to drive Angel Baby and her mom home that afternoon. When we dropped her off, I carried Angel Baby and her mom carried her things. When I handed Angel Baby off to her mom, Angel Baby cried. Really cried. I had to turn and walk out the door and get in my car. I heard her screaming as the door shut behind me.

I shut my car door and let out a "This is so hard!" It felt like my heart was breaking. The things swirling in my head said, "I'll do it for her though. Break my heart over and over. For her, I'll do it! God please, you are good, you are kind, and you are full of compassion. I know when she was born you had a good plan for her life, one with purpose, one where she would prosper. I will not give up praying and believing we will see this in her life. I will, however, sob now. I will miss her. I will miss waking up to her smile. Please Lord, I don't want to see the need for foster care to continue in Angel Baby's life."

These details are shared so you'll be aware. There's no part of this journey that I wouldn't do over again, but I will also not lie and tell you that it has been pain free, or that I don't question myself and my family's calling when I'm driving away from a baby who yells for me, and the pain in my chest fights with the truth in my head that God did lead me to be a foster parent.

Messages from God

During the time following Angel Baby's return to her mom, I watched a message by Bishop T.D. Jakes about "Feeding the Dream." I wrote down so many notes. It was as if Bishop T.D. Jakes wrote that message just for me. He said, "If you have a dream you can fulfill by yourself, it's not worthy of God." He went on to say, "This baby is too big to hold in your arms. You've got to be willing to hold the baby, feed the baby, and then give that baby back to God." That line made me tear up, because with our Angel Baby we held her, fed her, and then handed her back to her mom while telling ourselves that God still held her. With this in mind, I was able to move forward, encouraged for another day.[36]

How your fostering journey is going to play out will all be to God's glory, and it will only be done in his strength. Maybe there are more babies than you can physically hold that God will call you to parent at one point or another.

You may not want twenty kids in your house, but maybe he will ask you to hold that many in your heart. I don't know. What I do know is that one message, one text of encouragement from a friend or family member, and one step of faith at a time, will carry you forward even in the moments of fear, heartbreak, and doubt.

Weeks passed on. I heard a message by Charlotte Gamble that asked me, "Who are you in line for?"[37] I thought to myself, "I'm in line for Angel Baby and her mom." I was reminded in this message that you don't get out of line just because you are discouraged. You don't see the big picture and God does. Stay in line. Stay fighting for them in prayer. Stay in their lives. Don't let discouragement make you quit. Upon hearing this message I was again able to move forward, encouraged another day.

In the Bible there's a story about a twelve-year-old girl getting healed. On the same day there is a lady healed of a sickness she had been suffering from for twelve years. Jesus healed them both.[38] One person was healed on the day her parents came asking, and the other one was healed after twelve years of waiting. God will do what he promises. His timing may not be when we want it to be, but it's going to happen. Believe. Stay in line until you get that promise. Never quit because it looks different than you imagine. God has a bigger, better, and more effective plan than we can dream up. Our job is always to keep our eyes on him. We must remind ourselves of the promises he made us in scripture of hope, love, and faithfulness.

Circumstance can't distract us. His ways are higher than our ways, and he allows hard things that we would never choose. However, when we keep our eyes on him, we come out of those hard things stronger and more compassionate people, and more effective in the next task that he calls us to.

I can say that while looking back. But in the moment, keeping our eyes on God takes daily reading of his scripture to fight what you feel with the truth of his word. I've heard it put this way: "You don't have to like what you see, but you have to believe what you know."

Your first placement may stay forever, they may go home to family, or you may have to have them moved to another home for one reason or another. Just know that your God is with them. He loves them more than you do, and he also loves you. He will not forsake or abandon either of you. He does not disappoint. He cannot fail. He abounds in love and compassion. Run to him. He can handle every bit of the emotions, and all the questions, that come in these moments. In every moment, in every day, he is the answer that will get you to the next moment and the next day.

CHAPTER TWENTY-TWO

A Short-Term Stay

OUR FIRST PLACEMENT, who we called Angel Baby, was a short-term stay. She was with us for about two months. At the beginning of the stay CPS told us to expect three to six months. Believe me, two months is plenty of time to fall in love and feel heartbreak when they leave. It's also a great opportunity to support their family of origin. In this case, the mom was a former foster youth wanting freedom to do life on her terms with her child. I get that. CPS just wanted to make sure she could do that. The mom had to prove she had stable housing, income, and childcare. It was a true joy being her child's safe place while encouraging mom to get on her feet. I remember her saying something about her time in care and that she wanted something different for her child. I responded that she was already doing the hard work to make that a reality. And with her little one being so young, it was absolutely possible that her child would never have memories of being in foster care like this young woman did.

I'm proud to have gotten to meet Angel Baby's mom, and hug her biological grandma. I'm thankful to still get updates (usually I have to ask now, but Angel Baby's mom still responds) with a picture of our first love in her cheerleading uniform, or one of Angel Baby on her first day of big school. To be able to respond and tell her mom she's doing the good, hard work of parenting, and I'm proud of her, is a true honor. They don't live nearby, so we can't be a resource that is involved on a weekly or monthly, face-to-face level. However, I know some who do get to experience that type of relationship after their placement's case is closed and the child has returned to a parent or guardian.

The rest of our short-term stays have been either emergency placement for the night or respite. With respite, you are the caregiver while the full-time foster parent gets a break, goes on a vacation without the child because they don't have travel approval, or perhaps has a family emergency to take care of. We have enjoyed two, week-long respite placements. For one child, we knew nothing about them going into the week. For the other, we knew the family before taking in their child. With both, we went hiking. We played. We snacked. And we made sure that the girls (in both instances ours were toddler girls) had everything they needed and wanted for the week they were in our home. We spoiled them rotten.

Those types of stays let you love like I imagine a good grand-parent does–without a ton of rules because it's only for a short amount of time, with the goal of giving the child the time of their life. About the time you are getting tired, you get to send them home to their parents or full-time foster families. It's been a *ton* of fun for us.

Taking in emergency placements is when you'll hear hard stories. Their parents could have just been placed in jail, or a baby could have been taken at the hospital for drug exposure, parent murdered, or child was pulled from home because of suspected child abuse. I don't need to list all the ways a child is deemed in need of protection at the county level. With each child, I'm reminded that my daily struggles aren't as big a deal as I some-times seem to think they are. When you look at these innocent children, you find yourself wanting them to have every oppor-tunity the world can give them, while knowing that you only have this one night to keep them safe and loved. That will put life in perspective for sure. I find those times to be another overlook moment.

It's such a great opportunity to love with everything you have, meaning if it's a newborn, or a toddler who just witnessed tragedy, you can actually just keep them calm and happy and not get any sleep for one night. The life they are entering is going to be a lot, but you can give them all you have for the night or two CPS needs in order to find them a long-term home.

These short-term little ones are the ones that we love to take pictures of, find outfits and bottles for (whatever they don't already have with them and need), and write a note of encouragement to whomever is going to be on the long-term end of this journey with them.

We do our best, and provide for the person or people that are going to do the rest. We take pride in the fact that we now know this child, and we get to carry their name before God in our prayers for the rest of our lifetime. We also hang their pictures in our house and imagine the day that our paths may cross again. Then, we can bring them inside to see that they have been in our family ever since that one night we got to love them.

Whatever you can do or give, no matter how long or how little, it's not wasted. It's love.

CHAPTER TWENTY-THREE

Are We There Yet?
What's "The End" Look Like?

FIREFIGHTERS SPEND THOUSANDS OF HOURS training to learn the extent of their body's limits, their mental limits, and their equipment's limits. Yet, every one of them will tell you nothing trains you like experience. Firefighters are trained to recognize when a burning structure is too far gone for anyone to possibly be alive inside, and when to recognize there's a chance for survivors, in which case they are to enter and bring them out. Whether they choose to enter, stay out, or stop entering, lives are always at stake, and there will always be a voice that says, "Did I make the right choice?"

The same is true as a foster parent. Lives are at stake. Your life, the lives of those already in your home, and the lives of those you are welcoming in through foster care. We don't get thousands of hours of training. We aren't able to look at a building to see actual smoke and flames to signal it's time to stop going in. But we do still have that Holy-Spirit, gut feeling that says our time has come to an end here.

Know Yourself

You may find it is hard to say it's time to call it quits. You have loved what you have done for so long and your identity may feel tied to what you do as a foster parent. But God does not find your worth in what you do, but in whose you are. Your worth came at the price of his son. That price was paid whether you are a foster parent or not. Just because God used you as a foster parent doesn't mean God is done with you if you move on from foster parenting. God will have other good things in store for you. Psalm 139:16 says, "Your eyes saw my unformed body; all the days ordained for me were written in your book before one of them came to be." If God knows our days before we even begin, he knows the days we spend as a baby, as a teen, as a foster parent, as a mother or father, and the day that he will call us home. You've been obedient. Obedience doesn't equal the same role or area of service forever. This life adventure you're on isn't over. You're just looking for the next path forward.

If you feel like you're done, listen to your body. Take a rest from taking placements. If you need to have children moved out, then be honest with yourself, and allow yourself the grace to ask for their movement. Be honest with the children as well. Assure them the move is not because of them, instead because you have reached your limit, whether it be financially, physically or emotionally. None of us can go full throttle forever and if you are tired, you have to take a break. The children may be mad. They may be sad. They may act like they don't care. It will be hard. It will be painful. But that doesn't mean you don't need to do it. Only you will know when this point has arrived. Allow yourself to let go.

Know Your Equipment

Firefighters have fire extinguishers, special clothing, boots, and masks, not to mention everything on the fire truck. Foster parents have community, therapists, doctors, medications, counselors, and social workers. If you find yourself feeling worn out and questioning if foster parenting is still for you, I would ask whether you have reached the limits on your equipment. Maybe you need to ask for more help. Maybe a new tool needs to be introduced. Maybe the answer is personal counseling for you, microcurrent for your child or teen, or a few days of daycare or a mother's day out to give you a mental break for a few hours a day.

I would implore you to make sure you are using your equipment to its full capacity before considering that fatigue or frustration mean your time as a foster parent has come to a close. If it's physical fatigue that plagues you, have you mentioned this fatigue to your doctor? Maybe there are hormone issues or vitamin deficiencies to blame. With medication or supplements, maybe you could be back on track to feeling like yourself.

Sometimes we need to add in another piece of equipment, and explore the relief it provides to those within the walls of our home and inside the boundaries of our lives. I've included a packing list at the end of this book that makes mention of equipment you may not know of or forgot you had. Check it out.

Trust Your Gut

I've had periods where high stress, lack of motivation, and the needs of those adopted and not adopted all seemed to be too much. I have asked myself, "Are those signs that we are completely done fostering? Is my thyroid medication dose off again? Or is this just a really busy season where we need to rest from taking children in, but not quit all together?" PSA for women: the thyroid affects so much more than you may realize. Use those annual required physicals to get lab work done. Tell the doctor if you're fatigued or irritable and have them check if there are hormone levels at play and not just age."

When I find myself asking, Am I done? I do what I'm telling you. I check myself. I ask if I'm okay? If I'm not okay, what do I need to do to be okay? Am I using all the tools that are available, or that could be useful, in this time? Then, I tell my husband my doubts and frustrations and he asks me, "Courtney, can you really see yourself never having a new baby here again?" That's a gut check. Can I? So far my gut has answered, "No. I'm just mad, hungry, and tired." You may be mad or tired as well. Or you may answer that you just don't see yourself saying yes again, so why stay open? Trust your gut. If you can't say yes, don't say yes. But, if you can see yourself saying yes again, then keep your license for now. It doesn't hurt to have your foster parent license, but not accept placements for a time. It might frustrate a social worker at CPS who really needs a home for a child, but that's okay.

If your family can meet the forever needs of one child, that is enough. You don't put the whole family's future on the line because you feel a duty to keep going "into the fire." God has others he will walk with into and out of the fire. If it's time to spend the rest of your life in aftercare of the ones you've walked in for and out with, then you've done your job. Do not compare your family to others. Do not belittle yourself for *only* being able to help the number you were able to welcome. You were obedient when God said, "Go." And you went. You will continue to be obedient to who and where God calls you, and who knows what God has in store for you down the road. That's all he asks of you. Your God is not a God of shame and guilt, so if you feel those feelings, call them what they are: lies from the devil.

I believe this is a good place to remind us that we aren't the savior. If God chooses us to be part of a plan of redemption for one child or for many children, it is not up to us. We can make all the plans we want, have the best of intentions, but if God doesn't give us the strength and ability then we will constantly be finding ourselves fighting an uphill battle, which is when the high stress, irritability, fatigue, and lack of motivation all rise to the surface. It's only in being open-handed and saying, "God, I'm here to do what you would have me to do. I cannot and do not wish to go anywhere you are not calling. I'm believing that you will give me strength and wisdom so that I may be obedient to your call. When you say go, I'll go, and when you say stop, I'll stop." When we leave it all up to him, that's when we find the climb to be easier. We are not here to make a name for ourselves, although as humans we do love recognition for our hard work. If we are honored for the fifty-five years of service as a foster parent, but the last twenty years the children in our home could see the exhaustion and didn't feel the love, then we aren't listening to God. Yes, they may have been safe and fed, but were we operating in our gifting or were we just adding years to our resume?

We aren't here for gold stars, years served, or number of placements accepted. We are here for him, in his strength, and for his glory. Whether he has called you to one or one hundred, just make sure he is calling you still. Only then can you operate in his joy, peace, power, and timeline. If you have lost your joy and peace, maybe you are having a hard time letting go of something that has been good. That is normal.

Maybe God has a role for you to encourage those coming after you in the fostering world. Maybe it's loving your grand-babies. Maybe it's a completely new and unexpected adventure you or I can't imagine, but we won't know if we don't let go.

When Your Grip Slips

I was a homeschool parent for the first seven years of my oldest child's life. In the seventh year, it started to get less fun, but I resolved we just needed additional help. In the summer before the eighth year, I realized I had zero motivation, even with all the additional help and resources. I did not see a path forward in homeschooling. I had always said, "I'll take it one year at a time; we will see how long we homeschool." However, I secretly hoped and envisioned that I'd be able to send my kids off to college or their careers after having homeschooled the entire time. The summer of the eighth year was a different feeling. I didn't want to let go. I felt like a failure. I felt like I was letting my husband and kids down, so I could do what? I was doing everything I could to hold on, and now the grip was slipping away and I couldn't hold on. I didn't know what I would do if I didn't teach anymore, but I knew that the joy, the drive, everything that had been pushing me, was gone. So, I told my husband two weeks before school started "I quit. I can't teach them this year. Like at all." He was shocked, and overwhelmed with the short notice. My gut had been trying to tell me I was done all summer long. I knew I had reached my physical limits, and maxed out the equipment limits. I found myself having to give short notice because I had been unwilling to acknowledge what I felt slipping away from me.

My husband prayed. We looked at schools near us, but none were a good fit. We still had a son enrolled in dyslexia classes at our home that would interfere with traditional school hours. A lot didn't seem to add up to me being done. As the days ticked by, God unfolded a plan a little bit at a time until we had a real path forward. My husband and I both knew that only God could have made the path. It was a Red Sea kind of feeling. School began, completely online, with a lady coming to our home Monday, Wednesday and Friday, that had a master's degree in elementary education. On Tuesday, and Thursday we had an amazing young college student helping with the schooling, and teaching Mandarin (Chinese) to the girls. God had provided in ways we hadn't imagined possible.

If your grip has slipped, or if your time as a foster parent is ending, don't despair. God still has you. God is still leading you. Trust him to push the waters to the side, so you can see the path you are to walk now.[39]

CHAPTER TWENTY-FOUR

Reunification

THE FIRST GOAL OF FOSTER CARE is to reunite children with their biological family, whether that be the parents, a parent, or a kinship placement where the child is placed with a relative in the family. When a child is placed into the custody of the state, there will be a written plan with the goal being to get the child out of foster care. If there is a living parent, the goal will be written as return to parent. There will be things asked of the parent by the courts, whether that be drug testing, getting stable housing, or showing they can hold down a job and support their family. Over time, if these goals are met, the parent can go from having supervised visits with their child, to unsupervised, to overnight, and then have complete weekends with their child at home with them. If all goes well, the child and parent will be ready for reunification.

Reunification is hard, especially on the kids. They may have mixed emotions about going home and leaving new friends they have made, or trusting that it's okay to want to go home when the people who have been caring for you also love you. They could feel guilt, fear, and excitement all at the same time. The differing emotions could certainly lead to behaviors at home and in the foster home. There will need to be lots of open communication and support for them returning home, and acknowledgement of the normalcy of the feelings they are experiencing. If you have a good relationship with the parents and there is an option to continue support when the child goes home, let the family know you are willing to continue this life journey with them. Let them know you can babysit, or you'd love to still meet them at the park some days. Cheer them on! Building a support system so a family can be reunited and move forward together is the goal of foster care, and maybe that's the part you are passionate about. Just know, it will still be hard to see the little people struggle with their feelings, and you will have feelings to acknowledge and move through as well. That's OK, and it's normal. It's not a sign you are doing something wrong.

Be the In-Between Home

I know a young lady who was placed into foster care at the age of five and remained in foster care until emancipation at the age of nineteen.[40] I asked her, "Did you have any good homes in the fourteen years you spent in foster care? And what was the importance of the role those foster parents had in your life, even though they never turned into forever placements?"

She said there were only two homes that she would call good homes. Both were single parents. One was a younger mom, and the other an older mom. Both ladies showed her love. Both ladies attempted to go through the adoption process with her at different times, but as a child/teen it seemed like too much and this young lady called the adoption off at some point in the process each time.

Her advice to foster parents is to realize these kids have been through a lot, they have endured a lot, they have abandonment issues, and they also have normal teen hormones that affect their behavior and decision-making skills. She told me to "Try to be there as much as you can, talk to them as much as you can, but if they want to be off by themselves, give them the space to breathe too."

She says she is still in contact with both of the ladies to this day, and if she sees either of them she calls them mom. She says at the age of twenty-six she is still dealing with the effects of what happened to her as a child. She says the way that these ladies loved her is also still changing the way she is able to live today.

She never got reunification, and she was never able to go through with the adoption process. She says if she could go back in time, she would change the choices she made. She and I both hope that by talking about this you feel better equipped to love and support the children in your care. There must be a lot of grit and grace on this foster-parenting road. It's a lonely road to walk as a child, trying to make sense of all you are enduring. How do you move forward in life without a stable support system? How do you know who to trust? How do you even know what healthy relationships look like? How do you keep from believing that everyone that loves you is going to leave you at some point?

There are many children in need of people like you. Even if they don't allow you to adopt them, you still answer to mom, and you still pick up the phone when they call. Or maybe you aren't equipped to adopt them, but you are courageous enough to admit that this is your limitation, not theirs. Assure them you will always answer their text or meet them for lunch. You've heard from a previous foster youth that she would still call you mom. Would you assure her that she is still your daughter?

Providing Support to the Biological Family

My family said yes to a sweet little girl we will call Lucy. We were told by the social worker that there were family resources (meaning there were family members willing to take the child, but the paperwork hadn't been done to make that happen yet), so we should expect maybe a two-month placement.

I think Lucy smiled at me within the first five seconds of meeting her. Everyone that met her *loved* her. We met her birth family and loved them as well. We were all looking forward to being able to experience reunification for the first time. I sought out resources for the mom on attachment activities and practices because she was nervous about the time she was missing out on with her baby. At the first court date, the parents had done everything asked of them, and we were all expecting more visits, overnight visits, or something signaling that reunification was coming. For whatever reason, the court didn't change the orders at all, which meant it would be three more months before any changes would be made, and at that time it still wouldn't be directly to reunification.

My husband and I knew we couldn't maintain our house schedule, along with meeting Lucy's needs, once we realized this was going to be a much longer process than we had anticipated and prepared for. We chose to have the parents over and have an honest conversation about what was going on. I guarantee you I did not want to have to do this. I was so worried that they would feel let down, and that they would be hurt and angry that someone who looks like they have it together is now claiming they cannot continue to care for a perfectly wonderful baby. In all those feelings I felt they would be justified. I only hoped that being honest about my limitations would help them to feel better about themselves when they were faced with their own limitations at some point.

Pro-tip: eat first. Everyone needs to be in their best place before hard things are discussed. Do not have hard discussions when hungry, hot, or tired.

We ate biscuits and gravy, we talked about what it would be like to have Lucy back home, and then I got my computer, where I had typed out what I wanted to say. I told Lucy's mom and dad that on the surface I looked like I was doing okay because I was showing up for things and everyone was getting fed. However, I wasn't going to be able to continue for as long as Lucy was going to need me to. I told them I understood if they were mad, or sad, or both. I understood if they decided to not allow us to be in their lives anymore; however, I was hopeful we could keep walking this road toward reunification together, but not with Lucy sleeping in a bed in our home. I cried, mom cried, and dad reached over and held mom's hand.

Everyone hurts in the foster system, and everyone loses. But there can be beauty in the hurting together and losing together. If you keep your eyes on the One who called you, he will show you the beauty to be found alongside the pain. The weekend following Lucy's move to a new foster home, I was able to put my arm around my friend, Lucy's mom, and we were able to cry together. I told her I loved her, and it wasn't going to be like this forever. That opportunity was beauty inside of pain.

After Lucy's move, I kept in touch with mom via text and occasional phone calls. Eric and I continued to have Lucy's mom and dad join us at church, and several times we shared a breakfast together afterward. When court dates arose, I spent my morning with them at court. I wasn't allowed in the courtroom, but I was there as they waited, and I was there when they came out.

I didn't expect this to be the way I would experience reunification with a family, but it was truly not bad. I was getting to experience the highs and the lows alongside Lucy's family. On the days I knew they were going to have Lucy for her weekend visit, I texted with excitement, "It's Lucy Day!" I usually received a picture, or five, at some point during the time they were together, or after. It was a true joy.

I had my ideas of what it would look like to walk toward reunification with a biological family, and in none of them did I need to ask for their child to be moved to a new home before reunification. God works in mysterious ways. We treasured the time we spent with Lucy in our home, and we treasured the time we got to spend with her family after she left.

The family did move to weekend overnight visits, which meant the whole little family would show up at church together. I cannot tell you about the joy in my heart to turn and see that mom and dad, my friends and family now, walking and carrying their baby toward us with a big smile on mom's face, every bit as beautiful as her daughter's smile that I had fallen in love with originally.

If things don't go as planned on your road to reunification, be assured that God is still at work. He is never not at work. He never sleeps.[41]

CHAPTER TWENTY-FIVE

Adoption/Termination of Parental Rights (TPR)/Right Relinquishment

WHEN I BEGAN AS A FOSTER PARENT, I didn't know what the terms TPR or right relinquishment meant. They could have been the same or different. I had no idea. I just knew that at some point, some foster children get to a place where they could be adopted by the foster parent. I did know adoption meant the child would gain our family name, and they would be our child from that point on. I had no idea what it took to get to the point of adoption though. You may not either. I will begin this chapter with a brief explanation of what each of those terms mean, and how the child in your care could arrive at the point of being adoption-ready. Then I will move on to what experiencing Termination of Parental Rights alongside a child might feel like, and the same for adoption.

With the foster system you can have "right relinquishment" where the parents will sign away their rights to the child(ren). There won't need to be a trial to decide to take the parent rights, since the parent willingly signed away their right to the child. I haven't experienced that yet, but I know it's possible. I also know that even with right relinquishment, in the state of Alabama, it's not a quick process to get to the point of adoption. Be ready to wait.

We have experienced a Termination of Parental Rights judgment, often simply called TPR. This is when the court decides that every effort has been made to get the parent(s) to the place where they could provide a safe home for their children again, but the home environment is still unsafe.

Before the TPR trial, the court will also send out letters to the child's family members to see if any blood relatives can provide a safe home. In short, all efforts have been made to keep the family intact. But if the parents haven't complied, or were unable to meet the demands the court placed upon them, then a court date is set. At this point, the parents, lawyers, GAL, foster parents, and social worker(s) gather together and review all the information about the child's situation. The information gathered will be presented to the judge. The judge then decides if this case and the child it represents continue toward reunification, or if it's best to terminate parental rights and place the child in full care of the state. If the latter is chosen all of the rights to the child are taken away from the parents. At this point a child can be adopted by their current foster parents or through resources that have yet to be identified, such as other foster parents that are open to adoption, but with whom the child has not yet been placed.

TPR Trial Hearing

For us, the day of the TPR trial was so different from what I pictured. Just like everything in this journey, you have to go with the flow and can't hold too tightly to anything. The first TPR court date was pushed because of COVID. A few months later, at the second court date, we left without even knowing the result. There was no official announcement. Everyone testified. All the paperwork was piled in front of the judge. Then, when everyone was done, the judge said, "Thank you," and excused us.

I felt let down when I left. There was no finality like I expected to experience. When we pulled into our driveway my husband got a text. Yes, a text. The text read, "The judge said to prepare the TPR order." That's how we learned that the judge had decided our foster son was soon to be in a position for us to adopt him.

I expected to be happy. However, I felt his loss more than our joy. I hated that he was officially unbound to his birth family, or them to him. It was in his best interest, don't get me wrong, but it felt so sad and hard, and was not something I felt free to celebrate because I cared for his family too. I hated that they were in this situation. I thought of how it must feel to get this news and I hated the feeling those thoughts came with. Another loss. Another hard thing to add to the pile of hard things they had already experienced and faced. I once again just wished for heaven, and for all tears to be wiped away and all wrongs to be made right. I wanted them to be happy and whole, and then I would feel like I could celebrate.

My family was so kind when they heard the news. They prepared a meal for all of us to eat together. One of my sisters even drove in from out of state. We had all been waiting for this moment. We all prayed that if he couldn't be with his birth family, then Lord, please allow us to give him our best. There we were. We were going to get to do just that. Yet, I felt guilty that my family was excited and celebratory and I was feeling sad.

Friends and family sent breakfast, flowers, cards, and well wishes, knowing this would be an emotionally charged week. I shed tears, often feeling the love for us and for our baby boy, now a toddler, still waiting for his future to be decided for him.

I need to stop here and say that although it feels like men and women make decisions about the future of the children you love, you must hold tightly to the fact that God alone knows how all of this will play out. He is committed to drawing us to him. He isn't limited or hindered in his work in our lives, or theirs, due to a judge's decision. That belief is an anchor to cling to when it seems that people don't care enough, and they aren't making safe decisions for these precious children. I often prayed, "Lord, you alone have all the power to make all of this right. You alone can work all of this together for your good and ours."

After being told the TPR order was written, it was still four more months of waiting for different things to be checked off and completed. We contacted an adoption lawyer, we all got COVID, then we were advised to hire a different lawyer that was more well connected in the DHR world and knew how to do these types of adoptions. While we were home with COVID, we got on Zoom and met our new lawyer. We filled out paperwork, mailed paperwork, and about three months later we got to officially sign, for the first time, "our intent to adopt." We were so excited because for two and a half years we had the intent to adopt, should it reach that point, but there was nothing we could do to show that officially, until then.

Adoption Day

When I first envisioned adoption of our son we now call Jaxon, I thought we would all be in court, with all the friends and family that supported us looking on. We would pledge to love and care for Jaxon from this day forward. There would be tears and cheers.

Nope. COVID changed the picture. None of our family went to court, just the lawyer and the judge. We knew the date it was to happen and were told we would be contacted once it was official. Once again, my sister had come to town to support us. I am so thankful for the support on all these emotionally draining days. I had done homeschooling with the biggest three. I had done finger painting/handprints for our now youngest Fillebaum son to give to members of his biological family. I didn't feel cheerful. I felt stressed. I had agreed to meet up with his birth mom that afternoon. She wasn't aware it was his adoption date, but I was. She had told me she had gifts she wanted to give Jaxon and the others in his biological family that only I had visiting contact with. I had agreed to meet with her and pass along the things she wanted passed along. I felt obligated to do this, for her and for them, probably because I still felt the sadness of her loss. I had put too much on my plate and found myself suffering the effects of it.

However, we got the call, and of course my vehicle happened to be broken and in the shop. I had to ask for a ride to go meet the lawyer. I needed to pick up the papers saying the adoption was official. The lawyer met me near a 24-hour gym. I sat in the car, not knowing where she was. I let her know I was there via a phone call or text, but I can't remember which. She came out of an establishment, handed me an envelope, and that was it. Just a white envelope with three sheets of paper in it, the proof that Jaxon was now adopted.

Just a couple hours later, my husband came home from work and picked Jaxon and me up. We were off to meet with his birth mom. We didn't tell her what had happened that day. I did consider telling her, but I just couldn't come up with words that sounded right. Think about it. What do you say? "Hey, we adopted your son and changed his name today. You can still call him what you named him, but we are now calling him Jaxon." Or "Hey, I don't know if you know, but today he officially became ours. We kept the middle name you chose, but we changed his first name." It all sounded pain inducing to me.

You may find yourself in a similar situation one day, which is why I share the details of the way adoption, and interaction afterward, has played out for us. Hopefully these details and thoughts will allow you to consider the birth family's perspective, their ability to acknowledge what's going on, and what's best for them in the moment even if it's not perhaps what *you want* to do. *I wanted* to be able to hug mom and tell her that Jaxon was now Jaxon. *I wanted* to quit trying to manage switching back and forth between birth name, nickname, and adoptive name. *I wanted* to be able to celebrate *with her* that we (she, me, and Jaxon) were family forever. However, I didn't think his mom was ready for any of that. My choice of not bringing up adoption day was for her mental health, not my desires.

Four months before, I had gone to a court ordered "last visit" with Jaxon and his mom. I wasn't bound to have any other contact with her. On adoption day, this left me walking in uncharted waters. Jaxon's birth mom was always so positive, and for the most part she hadn't acknowledged the hardness of what she was having to do, or what she was experiencing. Even at *the last visit* she brought food and gifts, we took pictures, and she was incredibly upbeat. When I watched her that day, I was struck by the strength it must have taken for her to show up and keep an upbeat spirit for her child.

On adoption day, we told Jaxon's birth mom the new things that Jaxon loved, and made conversation as he ran around. She had gifts for Jaxon, and I had brought a few things for her as well. I wanted her to feel loved, and know that I thought of her, not just her son. When she said she had to go, I asked if she wanted a picture with Jaxon. (I still referred to him by the name she had given him. It was over a year before I had contact through text and chose to tell her his adoptive name.) Jaxon had taken pictures with her before, but for whatever reason on this day he did not want to. I placed Jaxon on my knee between us, and we took his first picture with him and both his moms–the first day he was officially not just hers, but ours. She didn't know, and I didn't plan it, but God did. I put that picture in his baby book. Our son. Hers and mine. I finally felt happiness, and peace, come over me as we drove away that day. I knew meeting her and giving her the gifts I had for her was the right thing to do. I was so thankful that I had gotten to share that day with her even if she didn't know the whole picture of what was going on. Maybe she would be able to be happier with the visit that way.

If you walk through adoption with a child, realize there are a lot of emotions that come with it. Although adoption is looked at by the outside world as joyful and something to be celebrated, adoption is also a huge loss. So, although we were walking into the future together, Jaxon still has a first family. We cannot, nor do we want to, take them away from him. Instead, we carry him forward, literally, and his family forward, in prayer, and in some cases even with contact and encouragement.

I felt Jaxon's loss on TPR day, and I felt his mom's loss on adoption day. If Jaxon was older, he would be the one trying to process those emotions. Be full of grace for your little or bigger ones on these impactful days. Be full of grace for yourself and your emotions as well. Just because the biological family isn't safe to raise them, doesn't mean your child doesn't carry love for them, or feel guilty or mad that they have to leave them. Family is messy. Love is messy. Believe it or not, our hearts can hold two families. Our hearts can carry sadness and joy. Our hearts can do more than our minds understand. I encourage you to be gentle with your words, ask God to keep you compassionate toward the birth family situation, and always look for ways to show God's love to your child and their first family.

CHAPTER TWENTY-SIX

Biological Family Contact After Adoption

"LOOK MOM! I HOLD TWO OF THEM." Jaxon, only three at the time, had his arms around two of his big sisters—one adoptive and one biological. I had the camera and snapped a picture of the three of them. I had braided their hair; we were spending the day at a park that we all love. It was the good and beautiful hoped for and found in the life of a foster/adoptive parent.

After an adoption is complete, it's possible that many people in the biological family will request contact with you. For us, it just isn't healthy or possible to keep equal contact with each family member. We keep in contact with the ones that we became closest to in the fostering process, and the ones that are the healthiest and best, at this point, for each other.

Even good meetups can bring stress to the whole family because it adds more to the calendar. There was one Christmas when a group meet-up was requested. I thought it would be fine. I felt obligated to Jaxon's biological siblings all see each other. Then a babysitter showed up instead of the other adoptive parents (Jaxon has siblings that were adopted by other families). The surprise babysitter changed the game for me. I was not made aware ahead of time that I was agreeing to give a new person access to my child, or allowing a babysitter to have pictures on her phone with my child in them. If I had been made aware, it might have been fine, I could have chosen not to come, or picked a time that the adoptive parents would be able to be present. Since I wasn't given a choice in the matter, I was frustrated.

Maybe you will be fine with a babysitter, maybe you won't. I'm just saying curveballs are going to come. It's okay and good to set boundaries for your family. When discussing meetups or inviting biological family to birthday parties or other such activities, I would recommend making a phone call or discussing it in person so words aren't attached to emotions you didn't intend when you typed a quick text. Don't be scared to ask specific questions about who all will be at this meet-up, how long are you expected to be there, and how often you are expected to do meetups like this. You can even say things like, "Hey, I'm inviting you (the birth mom for example), and I'd rather you not bring your boyfriend and his kids. I want you and your child to be able to have the most time together without others asking for attention as well." It's not mean. People will be less disappointed if expectations are discussed and set at the beginning. If you need to make changes as you go along, and you want to do more or less, just be honest with everyone involved. Of course, sometimes your requests may be ignored, and after a meet-up has happened, decide for yourself and ask your child, "Hey, was it okay that [x, y, z] came along with your mom?" If they are fine with it, and you didn't hate it like you thought you would, then let it go. If your child didn't like it, or it was too much stress for you, then when you are calm and able to be kind, make a call and speak to the person who brought the guests and tell them your concerns. They may promise never to bring extra guests again. They may get mad. They may explain why they did, and you can possibly gain understanding and compassion, at which point you can ask that they just let you know up front next time so you can prepare your child and yourself for the extra people. You may have to wait a while before you try to meet up again. Relationships require honest communication and work. This will be no different. You are capable of working for the good of your child and their birth family.

My other advice concerning post-adoption, and even before, is to always speak highly of the birth family to others and to your child. My typical response to others is, "They are doing the best they can at this time." The old adage "If you can't say something nice, don't say anything at all" doesn't just apply to your child's mouth. We adults could train ourselves to do the same. When you look for good in others, it can be found. "He is a hard worker," is something positive to say about a guy who was abusive, but took pride in earning a good income to support his family. Another is "Your mom loves you, but some people don't know how to show that or say that in a healthy way because it wasn't something she was shown as a child either." Those are just a couple examples that can be true statements. You leave out the things that weren't good. As your child ages, of course you will talk about the hard stuff, but only when they are ready and asking. Always circle back to "Whatever is true, whatever is noble, whatever is right, whatever is pure, whatever is lovely, whatever is admirable—if anything is excellent or praiseworthy—think about such things."[42]

You don't want your child to hear you speak of a family member in a bad light and think that you look at them through that same lens, or that they are doomed to be the sum of their parents' bad choices. It's crucial for your child to have hope for healthier and happier birth parents. Together you can pray for their healing and wholeness.

Set Boundaries

I love having contact with the sibling that we grew close to during the fostering period. It's good for both children to be around each other, and my other children love her and call her their sister as well. I'm sure the relationship will change as she ages and as Jaxon ages, and that's okay. Maybe they will get closer, maybe they won't. I hope they have each other to talk about the life Jaxon never lived, and the parents he never really knew. But if this relationship became unhealthy for either of them, then we would stop. They can always choose to reconnect in their later years.

Although I'm for continued family connections, I'm not for it without boundaries. The adoptive family should be making all decisions for the best for their child. If a relationship is not beneficial at any point, then you don't have to feel obligated to continue it. Do what's best for your child, but that doesn't mean separating them from everyone under the guise of "protection" from the hard circumstances that brought them into your home. Knowing the hard circumstances will be beneficial when it comes to them understanding why their story is what it is. But if your child will be harmed, or upset by visits at this stage, then no visits need to happen. Maybe you can continue the conversation by phone; just you and whomever wants updates. You can get to know them better, and they can be reassured that the child you've adopted is doing well.

It will be up to you to make every decision with your child and their future in mind. He or she will someday want answers about their birth family. So, to whatever extent you can, learn (especially good things) about them—even basic things like who your adopted child gets their eye color from, who is left-handed, whether a birth parent likes sports or music, or if everyone loves a certain snack food that your child desires all the time. Find pieces of their puzzle and save them for your child. Your child will appreciate it, and the family member that you gather information from should see that you're trying to provide family history and connection for the child, and not allow it to be washed away in the adoption. The washing away isn't possible for your child, so don't try. That will cause more problems when they are older. I love the show *Long Lost Family*. It's given me much insight into how an adoptee or a member of a birth family may feel years down the road. I suggest watching at least a few episodes, that way you have a clearer understanding of the impact felt when someone loses their biological family.

Who Can Keep the Distance?

I know someone who knows their biological family but only from a great distance. Because of this distance, the further down in the family tree you go, the worse the distant family is viewed to be. Why? Has that been told to them that this person is bad? I believe it's somewhat assumed because of the distance held for all these years.

Then the family got to meet the distant family member. They share eye color. They share likes and dislikes in foods. There are pieces of history held and known by this person that are valuable to the whole family. But no one knew. They just kept the distance.

You don't want to be the one holding the distance for your son or daughter. They will resent you for it. They are free to hold distance, because it's their heart they are trying to protect, but you cannot. You need to encourage them by saying there are good things in everyone, we just need to look for them. For a reason unknown to us, their family members were chosen to bring them into this world. Your child needs to know they are not doomed to become the things they don't like about their family any more than they are doomed to be the sum of every mistake their adoptive family makes. There are good and bad things about each of us. We are all more alike at the core than we are different.

All that to say, keep communication open when possible. Do visits when beneficial. Always, always, pray for and talk about the family in the best ways you can. If the situation isn't good, pray for their healing. Never, ever forget that hurting people hurt people. If they are hurting people, you can know they were hurt by hurting people and the cycle is continuing. As always, remember that at one point they were an innocent little baby and perhaps no one was there to keep them safe. Let's stop the cycle. Let's provide safety, and let's look for the good to be found in everyone.

A Mother's Day Letter

In some cases, there will not be the option or ability to either know of your child's family history or have contact with biological family members. In those cases, you still need to talk about the existence of birth family with your adopted child. Your child needs to feel safe to think about their first family, and to wonder if she or he is like them in any way. By *you* talking about their biological parents, your adopted child can never assume that speaking of the first family isn't allowed, or that it would be hurtful to you. You don't need to allow space for your child to write their own first family narrative, because it lends opportunity for your child to become *unwanted* in their own mind. It also allows what others ask of them to be *the truth* they believe. I've heard children and adults ask, "Did their parent just not want them?" To which I have always responded, "There are lots of reasons a person would feel unable to raise their child, but we are all thankful their first parent(s) still chose to give our child life." Your child needs to have worked through these thoughts with you before they find themselves answering the questions of others.

With you being open to speak about first family as soon as possible, your child's adoption is something they will always have known about. Your openness to speak of first family, allows you to help your child write a positive narrative. A narrative where you child is wanted, chosen, loved, and desired with their beginning not being allowed to wash those truths away. It instills confidence in your child that adoption isn't something to be ashamed of, or hidden, and it's also not a defining title over them. Adoption is just a piece of their story and nothing more. They still have much to write in their lives, that they will get to choose for themselves.

I can assure you that in my experience, your child has plenty of room in their heart for you to be their forever parent, and then still carry love or hopes and dreams for those who gave them life. There can be no competition if you are all on the same team, which is the team that is *for* your child.

I speak of birth family as often as I am given opportunity, and I create opportunities as well. One Mother's Day I took Anne Marie out on a dinner date. I brought along a notebook and pen. As we ate our dinner, I asked Anne Marie if she thought about her birth mom on days like Mother's Day. I don't remember her response, but I know that I told Anne Marie that I do think of her first mom. I think of the one that is missing out on watching her grow. The one that doesn't get her hugs or see her cartwheels and cat cuddles. I asked Anne Marie if she would like to write a letter to her birth mom. I explained that it would be a way to think through what she would want to know if she was ever given the chance to meet her first mom, and what she would want her first mom to know about her. Anne Marie readily agreed. The letter writing was my way to show Anne Marie that it's ok to think of her first mom, to ask questions, and to wish they knew each other. The Mother's Day letter was meant to reassure Anne Marie, I'm on her team, and her team includes the people that brought her to life, whether we ever get the chance to know them or not, they are still an important part of her.

CHAPTER TWENTY-SEVEN

We Are Family: The Journey Isn't Over.
It's Just Begun.

"WE SHARE THE SAME LAST NAME. After all the waiting, it's official. We are done!"

That might be what you think. Let me assure you now, that nope, you're not done. As you read in the previous chapter, after the adoption a new journey begins—the journey of learning how to share your heart, home, and future with not only this child but everyone they bring with them. Biological family ties, memories, and histories don't drop at the door of adoption. No. Now you are the one to help them carry their load for the rest of the journey. Shared suffering is a necessary comfort piece in adoption.

Anne Marie was only two when she cried because her eyes didn't look like mine. Jaxon was only three when he got angry at hearing he didn't grow in my belly. I didn't think at such young ages they would have strong emotions about these things. I was wrong. Once, I was looking through a magazine and the child with me said, "Is that my mom?" I stopped, smiled (caught off guard), and said, "No, that's not your mom." I have had people in public, in front of my children, ask about their ethnicities, or some other such "You don't belong" type questions. I'm not saying they mean well or ill, but these are things I have to be ready to answer anytime, anyplace. You may need to prepare for similar questions.

I want my kids to hear good things when it comes to their genetic makeup. I want them to be proud of their cultures of origin. How do I foster those attitudes? One way our family has tried is to speak highly of other cultures, not just theirs. We embrace differences. We love to visit places where the streets don't look like our street and the smells aren't like the smells in our usual bubble. We get on buses, we walk through towns, we meet people, we eat new foods, and we look for things we love in new environments. We talk about how people live differently in different states, countries, and even just as families. We talk about how being different is not bad.

How Our Alabama Family Travels

We live in the south. However, we decided on Anne Marie's 5th birthday that if China was a bit far for a birthday visit, then New York's Chinatown would be our next best choice. We rode the subways and the metro buses. We went to Chinatown twice. We walked through the Bronx on the way to the zoo. We found things we loved everywhere we went. When we were standing on the corner, waiting to cross a street in the Bronx, Kylen said, "Mom, I love it here. It's just so different. I love it." I couldn't have heard anything better. That's exactly how I wanted her to feel. That love and ease in being in new places doesn't come unless we put ourselves in new places, with a positive attitude, expecting to find goodness.

I took Anne Marie to a show that celebrates Chinese culture. We heard Mandarin being spoken, we saw many people that looked like her, and she saw Chinese words written on the banners that were hung. It was also *hot*. She probably doesn't even remember the heat, because we were too busy *loving* everything we were seeing and hearing. At the end of the night she said, "That was the best day of my life. Was it the best day of your life too, Mom?" I told her it wasn't because I got to experience China in person and meet her there, so I couldn't rate the night of the show above that. However, I did tell her it was *one* of the best days, for sure. Seeing how happy she was, and being happy with her–I just couldn't beat that.

Of course, there was a merch table at the show. Anne Marie picked out a necklace. The ladies behind the counter asked what part of China she was from and told her how beautiful she was. Then I took the necklace from the box and placed it around her neck. You should have heard the two ladies ooh, and aah. It was a moment for me. To think that I was able to be *the mom* placing a necklace around my daughter's neck, while these sweet ladies from her birth country looked on–it could have been so different. I was immensely grateful. It was one of the best nights of my life.

With Jaxon's birth family, we seek out seeing them when we can and when it's healthy for them. But outside of that, we seek to have friends and family that resemble those he could have been raised with. I don't want my brown-skinned babies to grow up in a community where no one looks like them. I didn't grow up that way, so why should they? I always want them to feel like they belong; so as much as I pray for that, I also try to create and give them that.

We don't exclude ourselves from any tables just because it might make me feel out of place. It's not fair to ask my children to live out of place but allow myself only places of comfort and familiarity. I have wild, thick, and curly hair. I used to straighten it a ton. I wanted to look like my sisters and the majority of the world I lived in. I had zero friends with hair like mine. It was a stressor trying to get my hair to behave like their hair. I clearly remember one rainy day–if you're curly haired in a humid climate you know this is not a good day for my hair–when I walked into a classroom of my peers. There was a certain gentleman who, upon seeing me, said, "You look like you got struck by lightning." Wow. I don't remember what I did, but I do remember the teacher trying to lead me through some calming exercises she knew. She said something like, "Imagine a door...what color is the door?"

If just having hair that's not like everyone else's is isolating, I can only imagine when it goes deeper into skin colors, eye colors, and ethnicities. I don't want to need to lead my kids through calming exercises. I want them to have had so many good experiences in their skin, and with people that look like them, that they have the confidence to weather and recognize ignorance for what it is.

Once, when we were driving through a rougher part of town, Holden asked, "Do bad guys live here?" I responded that bad guys live everywhere. They do. There isn't a part of town that is exempt from bad guys (or girls). The scarier ones to me are the ones hiding next door to you, disguised as an overly kind neighbor. I'd rather be around someone who has made some poor decisions due to a harsh upbringing and learned survival skills in the process, than someone who aims to con you with their charm and social status. I want my kids to know that a hard life lived doesn't mean "bad guy." And a charmed life lived doesn't mean "good guy."

I'm sure I don't do this raising-multiracial-children thing perfectly. No one will. They will know my heart though, and it's toward loving everyone, anywhere, and always. There are good, kind, loving families in every community and every country, and I aim to show that to my kids through the places we visit, the discussions we have, and the people we love. I would recommend you consider doing the same. You won't regret it. Your bubble may be cool, but there are so many other bubbles to be explored and enjoyed. If you've ever blown bubbles for a child, you know they are happy to run and pop just as many as you can provide. Have you ever seen them dance with the amount that comes from a bubble machine? Let's aim to fill their lives, and ours, with the joy of new and different experiences. Let's bring on the happy dancing.

Creating the View

You are curating your child's view of the world. Their view of the world needs to include people who look like them. Otherwise, they may decide that the only reason they belong in the world you live in is you. When they are older and don't have you by their side, they may feel as though it's not so obvious they belong, and to outsiders that may be true. Give your child access to their cultures of origin and people that look like them. Give them the knowledge (which comes with experience) that they can belong in any situation to whatever extent they want to belong.

What we do not know is scary. We can make up stories about what we do not understand. It is hard to love what you do not know and have not ever experienced. But God's nature is reflected in everyone. His image is on every face, and his love is for every race. We are the ones who get lost and make up beliefs about who these "others" are. That's not God.

It had been a little while since we had heard from Jaxon's mom, and I was finally able to get in touch and give her picture updates and ask about meeting up. When I told Jaxon about this interaction, he became angry. I asked why I couldn't talk to her and send her a few pictures of him, and he said, "No, I don't love her!" I said, "I understand it is hard to love someone that you do not know." He calmed and asked me, "Do you know her?" I said, "I do." He replied, "Tell me." I took time to remind him through words and pictures who his birth mom is. When I finished he said, "I know her. We can meet up."

It's harder to hate someone you know. The learning, and loving, has only just begun. You're family now. Time to act like it. Traditional families are people who look alike, love some of the same things, and protect each other. Your family may not look exactly alike, but you can create an extended family that reflects your children. Creating this extended family and community takes time. It takes effort. It is necessary. It is worth it.

CHAPTER TWENTY-EIGHT

When You Don't Know How It Ends

ERIC TOOK ISAIAH BACK TO DHR. They wouldn't even let him meet whoever Isaiah would go to. We had to walk away from Isaiah being in our home, and not know the ending. But there are many times in foster parenting when we don't know the ending, like when the mom is pregnant again, and only just got her first child back. Or, the birth mom is pregnant again and hasn't gotten the other children back yet, and their dad is in jail. The birth mom might move a new guy in to be "dad" and help get her life back together. A child may overreact to a seemingly small issue and the foster parent has to call 9-1-1 to report a runaway youth. Or maybe it's the beginning of a day meant to be spent with a close friend and our combined eight children, when I walk out the backdoor and break my toe on a scooter I didn't see.

We look at these situations and we wonder how these stories end. Will it be good? Why does it seem to be getting worse and not better? Is anything we do even making a difference? What is my part in the problem, if any? Am I just supposed to pray? Can my eyes be opened to see God at work in situations where I don't see him? Do I need more faith when I do not see what God is doing?

I find myself wrestling with questions like these even still. I wonder about those I knew and loved. I wonder where they are now, and how life is going? I wrestle over the undesirable appearance of situations that I do know about. It's hard loving so much, and having so little actual control. It's good, however, because if we were in charge, and the people we love were making the choices they are making, or having choices made for them that we don't desire, we would feel fully responsible to fix everything for everyone. We all know we can't even fix our own situations to the extent we would like. We all need God and his wonder-working power for incarcerations, unplanned pregnancy, teen pregnancy, substance abuse relapse, physical abuse, and the many other unwelcome struggles and truths found in the lives of those touched by foster care. Maybe that's the point. Maybe we need to realize and embrace our dependence on him.[43]

I would love to put each foster care experience into boxes marked "success", "miracles", "good choices lead to good results", and "bad choices lead to bad results." Instead, I have a box in my mind marked "I don't understand." The number of situations I've placed in that box keeps growing. I tell myself I never know the inner workings of God in each and every person I love. Maybe I can trust that God is still working even though what I see looks like someone was really trying to do good, but life is still going bad for them. But often I find myself trying to make up a story I'm okay with. A story that leads me to believe that if I do good, it will be good. That's just not true. The more I live the more I see, and sometimes you do good and there are still bad results. I can't dwell on that too long though. I have to keep being faithful to the people and places God calls me to and let the results be what they are. Trust God with *all of it*. We don't have to understand the endings, but we have to trust the God who led us to that ending.

In some of the stories being written in the lives of children and their birth families, you will get to see God clearly at work. In other stories the endings may outlive you. Our job isn't to create good endings. Our job is to trust the Author and Perfector of faith, be obedient when and where he leads, and trust obedience is our part.[44] If our love, and our investment in someone's life, doesn't lead to their acceptance of God's love and sacrifice, it doesn't mean we did the wrong thing, or we didn't love them well enough. God left us all with free will. Unfortunately, some people will not choose him, and others will wait until the very last second to choose him. Let's be the people committed to reaching those last-second hands out to the hurting, no matter what, no matter how many times we have been rejected before. Let's keep believing and reaching toward them. If it's not us that gets to help them at the end of the road, God will send someone else to offer a second, third, or fiftieth chance to turn all those bad choices around.

Hope

I believe God is ok with me asking for what I desire for each of my children, but sometimes a child might not do well, and other times, or other children, are going to do well. I do not get credit for either of those. What I do get is hope, as long as I am doing what he has asked of me. Hope is the difference between life and death. Without hope, you and I would perish. Why would we continue forward in any hard thing if we knew there was no hope that the situation would change or get better?

Hope deferred makes a heart sick, the Bible says.[45] If our heart is sick, there is no joy and no life. But in a terribly hard situation that we could otherwise not survive, if there is hope there is not only a chance of survival and life after the current situation, but also life *in* the current situation.

Have you ever seen a parent or guardian with true joy, even in the midst of their child's life-altering battle with sickness or a fatal disease? I have. Every time it's because they were a believer. A believer in miracles, a believer in the goodness that still existed in this hard place, a believer that they would be able to comfort others and use this to bring ease of pain to someone else. The goodness they looked for and saw was found by them in little ways, if not in big ways. The same is true for you. Never let go of hope. Never believe that the hope of a good forever is over and nothing good will come from a hard situation. Change may not come for that child, but your strength in hardship may be a changing force for another parent in a similar struggle. I don't know. You don't know. But if we hold onto hope, we will develop the strength to endure. Maybe the ability to endure is a superpower of its own. Endurance is fueled by hope, I know that.

I spent a few weeks working in an emergency room as a respiratory therapist in training. An older guy came in one day. He had been brought via a life flight helicopter from a car wreck. The medical team met him on the roof of the hospital. His head was laid open. I could see a pretty big piece of his skull. I was in charge of holding his head still while the team assessed his needs. I stood there, amazed, that he was cognizant and answering questions. It seemed to me like he should be out of it or screaming in pain. Your situation, or your child's situation, will be much like this at times. It's an ER day. The situation is hard. It seems like we should all be screaming (maybe sometimes we are), and we certainly need a whole team assessing what we need and making a plan to meet those needs. Just remember, no one stays in the ER forever.

We don't know what God will do with the unplanned pregnancy, what he will teach us when we literally can't run from our problems because our toe is broken, or what he will do in the lives around us that seem to be falling apart. We can however, be bearers of hope. We can endure. We can live expectant and not defeated.

Get Your Limp On

I wrestle some days more than others. Just because you wrestle doesn't mean your faith is weak. It's okay to wrestle with God. Jacob wrestled with God and walked with a limp the rest of his life.[46] It's okay to limp as long as we are still walking with God. Our limp is an outward call to those who feel like their hardship is a sign a loving God doesn't love them. If they see that we too limp, we too struggle, yet we too walk with God, then that limp is the sign that they are welcome at the table as well.

Believers have a bad reputation of teaching and following a thought process of "A good believer gets good things. A good believer with faith will move mountains, so if the mountains don't move then it's on you. Your faith is weak." That's just not true. We can believe and we can wrestle. The mountains don't always move, but we need to believe that they can. Then when they don't, we can wrestle with God about that. He will reveal himself to us sometimes, and other times he will be silent. It's up to us to choose to still believe and continue to limp *with* him along the road we are following.

Many of us limp, but many of us don't let the world see it. We are too afraid it shows our weakness, too afraid others would be disappointed, or too afraid that it's a disqualifier for believers. It's not. Get your limp on. People will find themselves wanting to be you. They will want to know how you can struggle, and still choose to limp forward. Tell them. It's God making himself strong in our weaknesses. That's what he longs to do. Let him. Be honest with yourself. Be honest with others. Be honest with God. He can handle it.

Move forward another day. That's all you can focus on when the ending is unclear. One moment at a time. One day at a time. Get up and move. No matter how you feel, your God is still there. You can't see him? He didn't leave. Keep putting yourself next to him and one day you will see and feel him again. Just don't walk away under the illusion that he left you. He never has, because he never forsakes.

CHAPTER TWENTY-NINE

Will We Go on Another Trip?

AFTER A LITTLE ONE LEAVES, you can take some time to rest, and acknowledge both the hard and the good parts of this work. Do something for yourself and your people. Don't declare you're done because this hurts too much. It *will* hurt too much. You are also capable of healing. Don't jump into another placement in order to mask the pain.

When our first placement left, we headed to the beach for a couple of days. It was wintertime so we took our homeschool books and just enjoyed each other and the change of scenery. When the next call came, we didn't say yes. We weren't ready yet.

Please let yourself say no. Let yourself have a break. Let yourself not be okay if you need to. Make sure everyone has time to heal from the work and the emotions just spent. Don't rush into another placement in order to avoid dealing with the aftermath of what just happened. There's no specific time period that's right for healing. Take the time you and your team need. It could be a month, or it could be a year. You'll have to figure out what's right for you. Just listen to your team and listen to yourself.

When we moved into our new house after our year-long placement that didn't end in a way I desired, I wasn't sure when I would be ready again. When I felt like maybe I was getting to a place I could say yes again, we said yes to a respite placement. That went really well and I felt like I was ready to do a long-term placement again. So, over the following month we said yes to several potential placements. However, in one case they placed the child somewhere else. In another case, the current foster parent decided to keep the placement. I don't know what happened with the third, but the child never showed up. I was upset that each child wasn't there. That showed me that I was ready! These experiences built my anticipation level for when a child would finally arrive.

We finally got a sweet little dude straight from the hospital. He was precious! His case worker said that we should expect this to go to adoption since the child's parents were already facing the Termination of Parental Rights for a sibling older than him. We thought, "We are probably looking at a forever son!" Within twenty-four hours the little dude was gone. He was handed back to his mom, and my kids were sobbing. That was an emotional roller coaster.

On the first and only night, before he was returned to his mom, I sat in the closet and cried as I fed him a middle-of-the-night bottle. I was suddenly panicked that I wouldn't be able to meet his needs, and I would break everyone's hearts by sending him away in the end. My mind was screaming, "You were wrong. You weren't ready!" I was reliving what I thought I had worked through, and I was so, so scared that I was about to experience my inability to keep a baby for as long as they needed me all over again.

I didn't know how to process that panicked experience when the little dude was given back to his mother. I thought maybe it's what I got for freaking out on night one. I blamed myself. I had hung a little sign in the baby room that said, "Enjoy the moment." I hadn't truly enjoyed the moment. I panicked in the moment. I told myself that if God gave us another chance with a little one, I wouldn't jump into the future in my mind. That experience showed me that no matter what I thought, I may only have a few hours with a child and I didn't want to waste any of those hours crying over the possibility of something that might not even happen. I was resolved that the lesson was learned, and I would stay present with the next one. Little did I know that God was preparing me for a two-and-a-half-year walk and an ending of adoption with the next *little dude* to make an appearance at our door.

If you aren't sure you are ready for another road trip, it's okay. There have been ebbs and flows in the energy in our family and the desire to say yes, or to admit we aren't ready. We stay "readied up." We do our home visits to keep our home open for placements. We get our physicals, we get flu shots, and we answer the phone when it rings. Tomorrow may be the day that we all get the feeling that another child is supposed to enter and we are off on another trip down the foster-parenting road. Tomorrow may also include us reaching out to the birth family we are already committed to, or a talk with Jaxon and Anne Marie about their birth families. All of those tasks are to be found on a family's walk as adoptive and foster parents.

You know the need is great. You know that there are never enough good homes, but your home won't be a good home if you say yes to more than you are ready for. You must rest. You must listen to yourself. If you want to be life giving, and you want to stay the course, you can't say yes every time, and to everyone. You will end up worn out and bitter, find yourself living the life of the local who has such beauty within walking distance of the front door but in twenty-five years has never stepped a foot toward it. Why would they? The beauty is always there. They have decided it's not special because they aren't living a life of exploration and admiration. They aren't tourists. They look down on the tourists who drive slowly and take it all in, and possibly even say, "Looooosers." I don't want the local life for you. I want you to enjoy the drive, know the caution signs, and be confident you belong on this foster-parent (family) road.

Just because you belong in the foster parent role doesn't mean you won't doubt yourself. The greatest people with the greatest skills aren't above doubt and pressure. Olympic athletes, authors, doctors—you think they all just walk around fully confident they are above mistakes and weaknesses? No. They doubt themselves too. They question themselves too. However, they find that the task at hand is worth the battle of the mind to complete it. They aren't quitters and neither are you.

If you have ever taken a test you weren't prepared for, you know the results are likely a bad grade, if not failure. Let's not sign up for a test we aren't ready for. We can ace the test when we are properly rested, fed, and raring to go. Let's set ourselves up to be good test takers, for our sake, and for the good of the child(ren) who will be counting on us.

Let's go into the next placement with excitement and anticipation, but let's also go in knowing we aren't the answer. The watching world will say you're special, or a hero. You're not. Your God is. He did put a special burden on you, to enter this foster care world, and for that, I'm excited.

I just want you to keep the passion and do a great job. Set some rules and boundaries, be honest with yourself about what you can really handle (God will give you more than you can handle. Don't worry about not signing up for enough. Just worry about signing up without him co-signing), then get going! This will be fun! This will be the greatest adventure of your life. You will see and be part of some amazing things. You can spend a lifetime doing this work. You will have great joy.

Are you up for the task? I think you are. Your God will be with you. He goes before you to prepare the way. He is the one who parted the Red Sea. He allowed Jonah to be swallowed by a fish to get him to go where he was supposed to be going.[47] Let's not make God create a land whale to come find you. Let's go where he is calling with humility. Let's go knowing we are going to *need* him in order to be successful. Let's go, giving him all the honor. Let's just GO!

CHAPTER THIRTY

To the Baby that Started it All

Waiting For You

I bought you an outfit (maybe three)
I bought you a blanket
It was white with green

You were wrapped in a blanket
Arm bearing a bracelet
I met you in my dream

I chose your name
I told my family and friends about you
I took classes to qualify myself to find you and hold you

Bought a car seat
Put together a crib

I was ready

Where are you?

I've answered the phone calls
Always wondering
Will the call be about you?
Is this the day of your birth?

I've met and loved many because of you

But never you

Are you real?
Are you a mirage?
A hope to pull me forward for a very good cause?

Some days my arms are so full
I get scared I can't hold you
Do I have to let go?

Name
Preparations
Dreams
All I hold

Waiting
Hoping
Dreaming

Forever grateful for you
My dream baby
To me you will always be true

To all who dream, keep dreaming. To all who hope, keep hoping. It's better to spend our lives actively loving others while waiting and dreaming of more to come, than it would be to risk having our backs turned when the promised one arrives.

While I have waited for my dream baby, I have found there are many dream babies, but they are not all meant to be mine forever. All of these children are waiting for hearts to be turned toward them, eyes to behold them, and arms to comfort them while we all journey forward to the One who calls to us all.

I thought this book would be written after I met my dream baby. I thought my fostering road would lead to her. However, I believe now that the road was always meant to lead to you. You, the moms and dads, that will follow those who have gone before you. You who will get on the road towards loving children, and the families they come from, during some of the most crucial points in all of their lives.

I hope I have left you feeling equipped. I hope I have left you encouraged. I hope you will let me know when you find the one(s) that God has prepared you for.

Much love to each of you, from a fellow traveler.

A Packing List for Current or Future Foster Parents

You will not need all of the following resources before you begin your foster care journey, but it might be helpful to engage these resources while you have time and are in the waiting period. Imagine this section as the suggested items for a road trip of this sort. You may not need them all, or you may find some must-have items that you add to this list. This is my list of "items" I wish I'd had or found useful along the way.

Professional Training

Once you become licensed, there's a certain amount of Continuing Education Units (CEU) hours that you will be required to do yearly. I recommend seeking out CEUs that are helpful to you in your current season, such as a training module that addresses the struggles you're facing with the children you are currently helping. Don't just listen to or join anything to get the box checked. These required hours can be a required godsend. A good CEU can be like a glass of cold water when you're on a long, hot hike.

I recommend CEUs offered by Lifeline Children's Services, currently the largest Christian adoption agency in the US. They keep an archived list of CEUs and if you get on their mailing list, they will send you links to live CEUs in which you can participate in the question-and-answer time. More times than I'd like to remember, I have had tears falling because the people speaking were such a breath of fresh air. They spoke to my situation and understood what I was facing. They encouraged me and gave me practical tips on how to do what I was doing even better. The hour spent with them left me feeling like not only was there a path forward, but that I was equipped and able to walk it. Find a list of CEUs at

https://lifelinechild.org/event-category/ceus/

I also *highly* recommend "Hope for the Journey." It's the newest recording of the previously known training, Trust Based Relational Intervention (TBRI) by Karyn Purvis. This training helps you to avoid labeling a child by surface level behaviors, and instead see that he or she needs something from you that they aren't getting or didn't get. Only when those needs are met is a child going to be able to listen to what you may need from them. It also contains practical advice, such as regular snacking and drinking, and the importance of how basic things like sleep and nutrition affects our brain and our ability to function well.

"Hope for the Journey" has been a helpful and applicable way to approach parenting with all of my children and all of my relationships, close or in community. This way of interacting with people is so much healthier than just raising kids the way you may have been raised. I'm so thankful for the way this approach and shift in perspective has allowed me to meet my children where they are, and parent them more effectively. It takes a lot of intentional training on my end, but it's worth every bit. I see the benefits. I wish everyone who interacts with children on any level could experience "Hope for the Journey." *All of it* is so good. You need to do this training now, and then again, a few years in. You could do it yearly and come away with different nuggets depending on the situations you are in at the time you watch it.

In the state of Alabama, each parent is required to do fifteen hours of CEUs to remain licensed. The first year, all of the classes you do to get licensed meet that need. After that, you can choose to attend training courses given by local agencies, go to conferences, or join online virtual lessons. You can also choose to watch movies and write a report on how it relates to fostering, or read books and write a report of the same kind. (Hey, if you are already fostering, you're welcome! This book could be good for a CEU!) Water safety classes and CPR classes count as education hours as well. Some counties may require you to be CPR trained every two years. Repeated CPR training is not the most exciting time, but incredibly important should a loved one need it!

My advice is to pick CEUs that apply to your current situation. If you don't have teens yet, why waste time freaking out about those years? If you have concerns already, go ahead and look for training sessions. They are not created equal, so if you need to bail and find something more helpful, do it.

Professional Counseling

Eric and I have benefited from going to counseling and I would implore you to be open to the idea as well. It can be done separately or together, for the marriage, for dealing with secondary trauma (the trauma received by constant exposure to traumatic stories or being up close to individuals experiencing trauma), or for family counseling where perhaps children are involved at times as well.

There are counseling options available via virtual appointments now, so you can take away the excuse of an office or therapist not being close enough or convenient enough. We have done in-person, but we have had a lot more virtual appointments as that worked with our schedules more easily.

The counselors really must be trauma informed, and it would be even better if the therapist has had close dealings with children who have been in foster care, or institutionalized (orphanage) and adopted. The outside world cannot understand the inner workings of these traumas and how trauma can affect the individual and those loving and raising them. Asking for recommendations for therapists/counselors in online adoption or fostering support groups would be my first go-to for finding who and what services are available near you. If you're in central Alabama, I recommend any of the staff at Noonday Therapeutics. My family and I have been positively impacted by their practice. We have also benefited from a family counselor that we were guided to through staff at Lifeline Children's Services.

What I would not recommend is thinking everything a *professional* says is the correct path forward for your family just because they have credentials behind their name. You are still the one closest to the action. Therapists will even say that each relationship is different based on the nuances of you and your family makeup. Once, I tried to save money by finding a therapist on a website that was not trauma- or adoption-educated. I thought since they were just being asked to counsel me, it wouldn't matter if they didn't understand everything going on around me. I was wrong. A lot of my stress is related to the things going on around me. One day when I was asking for some sort of calming exercise the counselor said, "Let the child scream and tell them when they stop, you'll come back." Well, that just can't be done with a child who has experienced abandonment because it would only increase the fear and the screaming. I told the counselor such, and she was kind and said she understood; however, there were other comments that were similar and I saw this wasn't going to be a resource I could use. If you need someone to tell you that you don't need credentials to know that further traumatizing your child is not a good choice, here I am telling you to find someone else to help you. Sometimes the best help comes from the other adoptive and foster moms on the road. They may have tips and tricks you haven't learned yet. Admitting you need help is not a weakness, it's wise.

Your Home Library

Stock your home library with children's books that will reflect the cultures of the children to come. You may want to do the same with the toys you buy. I have a doll set that includes little dolls reflecting different nationalities. You will want the children that enter your home to see themselves in the books you read and the toys they play with.

An important book for you to read is *The Body Keeps the Score* by Bessel van der Kokl, MD. If you want to learn about yourself and others, read this! It will dispel the notion that if you get a child young enough, they won't be able to remember the bad things that happened to them and they will be perfectly fine as they grow and won't need additional help. Your body *always knows*. It keeps score, and sometimes the not knowing is worse because you don't know how to treat what you can't make sense of.

Get and read the book *Tear Soup* by Pat Schwiebert and Chuck DeKlyen. I give this book to everyone! Have it on hand. Read it with your kids if you're processing a goodbye. It helped me see my stress and anger for what it actually was—sadness and grief. I didn't realize I was grieving and thought instead I must be losing my mind. This book is so well illustrated and gives resources at the back for places to learn more on how to grieve well, and how to comfort those who are grieving. It includes great resources for kids and adults. It's also a simple, kid-sized read—less than fifteen minutes long. It states as its purpose on the inside cover of this book "affirms the bereaved, educates the unbereaved, [and] is a building block for children."

Instruments in the Redeemers Hands by Paul David Tripp is another great resource. This book is one to highlight and refer back to. Tripp speaks so well on how we, as broken people, can effectively be an instrument in God's hands for healing in another broken person's life.

The Whole-Brain Child by Daniel J. Siegel, MD and Tina Payne Bryson, PhD was recommended by our play therapist in hopes that I will better understand my children and parent them in a more effective and understanding way. It includes comic-looking illustrations of interactions between parent and child with "instead of this...do this." They are not hard concepts, or difficult things to do, but the concepts are not something I even knew I should be doing. The two authors are phenomenal. They aren't saying "Hey, you've been doing terribly," but they are saying "Hey, you didn't know all this brain stuff, so let us show you." Then you can see why what you've been doing hasn't been working. Also, here's what to do that will work. This book has been so helpful.

A Love-Stretched Life by Jilliana Goble is another great story about what a life can look like as a foster care family. I like the honesty she wrote with, and the hope. If you are trying to get a broader picture of what foster parenting could look like, this book is another foster/adoptive mom's perspective and experience.

The Connected Parent, by Karyn Purvis PhD, and Lisa Qualls, is a very applicable read for any parent, but especially a foster/adoptive parent.

I would also echo my husband Eric who says, "Don't go to a ton of training and load your toolbox until you can't even pick it up." Just like you can't help every kid, you can't implement every tool at the same time without overwhelming yourself or quitting before you even begin. Don't overthink what foster parenting will look like for you and your family. Just know that there are resources available when you need them.

Additional Resources

If you are having thoughts of suicide, or the world being better without you, please talk to someone now. This is not the time to be worried about what anyone else may think. The world is better off *with you in it*. We need you here.

In the US, call or text 9-8-8 to reach the suicide crisis hotline, available twenty-four hours a day, seven days a week. Or use the chat at 988lifeline.org/chat. Services are free and confidential.

Glossary

Adoption: the action of legally taking another's child and bringing it up as one's own, or the act of being adopted.

Child Protective Services (CPS): state-operated service that provides for children who are at risk of, or are experiencing, neglect, physical, sexual, or emotional abuse. The focus is on the safety of the child and support for parents to strengthen families and promote safe, nurturing homes for children.

Continuing Education Units (CEUs): CEUs are awarded by many education and training providers to signify successful completion of non-credit programs and courses intended to improve the knowledge and skills of working adults. (They are required yearly to keep your fostering license.)

Court date: a date, set by the court, when your child and their biological family will have their case reviewed by a judge and the lawyers. In the state of Alabama, cases are reviewed every three months, sometimes sooner if conditions have changed and lawyers request for a case to be reviewed earlier.

Department of Human Resources (DHR): another term (especially here in Alabama) used to refer to the state-operated service/organization that provides for children who are at risk of, or are experiencing, neglect, physical, sexual, or emotional abuse. The focus is on the safety of the child and support for parents to strengthen families and promote safe, nurturing homes for children.

Guardian ad litem (GAL): an individual appointed by the court to look after and protect the interests of someone unable to take care of themselves, typically a minor or someone considered legally incompetent.

Group home: residence intended to serve as an alternative to family foster homes.

Individualized Service Plan (ISP): the ISP is intended to bring everyone (foster family, GAL, case worker, and biological family) together to address the unique needs of your family. It is meant to identify the specific services that will be provided to your child and family so the safety and well-being of the family members can be achieved.

Licensed: refers to a person or family that has completed the training, the paperwork, and the home visits required in order to obtain a license from their state saying they are approved to have a certain number of foster children in their home of a certain age.

Long-term stay: when I use this term, I'm referring to a child that is placed in your care for a year or more.

Placement: when a child or children are officially placed in your home as your foster children. You will have a "placement" letter that states who they are and where they are being placed as proof they belong in your home for a certain amount of time (yet to be determined of course).

Respite care: this care is to provide foster parents a planned break. If you are providing respite care, the child(ren) is only placed with you for a few days or a week depending on the reason for the break needed by the foster family. If you are the parent asking for respite care, your social worker can find another foster family to keep your child should you need a mental break, or a visit out of state where the child hasn't been approved to travel, etc. The child will be returned to you at the end of the respite weekend or week.

Right relinquishment: the act of the biological parent(s) signing paperwork to willingly give up the rights they have to their child(ren).

Short-term stay: in this book I refer to a short-term stay as any stay less than 6 months, whether it be an emergency overnight stay; a week-long, in-between-homes stay; or the placement of a child that is with you for a few months.

Supervised visits: when supervised visits are ordered by the court, the biological family can see their children but only when supervised by someone the court has deemed able to do so. This could be the social worker, the transport driver, or in some cases even the foster parent.

Termination of Parental Rights (TPR): when a parent loses their parental rights, they no longer have any right to live with or even see their child. There is no legal right to visitation after termination of parental rights. The only way for the parent to maintain contact is through permission of the legal parent(s) or guardian(s).

Therapeutic Foster Home (also called Treatment Foster Care or TFC): care that is provided by foster parents with specialized training to care for a wide variety of children, usually those with significant emotional, behavioral, or medical needs.

Traditional foster home: a home with a parent or parents that is or are licensed to provide care for a child or sibling group that has been placed in state custody for an undetermined amount of time.

Transport drivers: people who are paid to pick up children and transport them to and from activities, foster homes, and biological visits. Sometimes the transport driver is even tasked with supervising the visits.

About the Author

Courtney Fillebaum is a wife to Eric, a stay-at-home mom to four forever children (currently), a resource parent for Big Oak Ranch, and a co-owner of a martial arts studio serving children in her community. She grew up in the inner city and saw many children experience a childhood much different than her own. She desired even at that point to bring children in and give them the safety and love that she experienced in her family of origin. Today, she and Eric invest in kids in several different avenues. The one that is closest to home is having the ability to share their home and family life with little ones and their birth families. She, her husband, and her children became a foster family in 2016 and they say, "It's what we do." Find her on Instagram @fillebaum, or at courtneyfillebaum.com.

Acknowledgments

I have to first thank God for telling me that writing a book could be part of my fostering journey. I had never considered writing for anyone but myself until the day I heard him speak to me. I have found much hope and excitement in the fact that God chose to use me to encourage the next generations of foster parents. Next, I need to thank my husband Eric for the constant encouragement to do what I feel called to do. Outside of God, he is my earthly rock, and my very best friend. I also have to thank my favorite kids in the whole wide world: Kylen, Holden, Anne Marie, and Jaxon. They follow in their dad's footsteps when it comes to their ability to encourage me and speak truth to me when I doubt myself.

This book would not have become a reality without all the friends and family who agreed to read it in its earliest and roughest stages. I will be eternally thankful that you didn't tell me the book was awful, and instead you gave me positive feedback which led to my continuing down the writing road. That list of tremendous people includes: Angela and David Anderson, Camille Arrington, Tara Barger, Jennifer Bradford, Martha Ann Clark, Jamie Clayton, John and Judy Fillebaum, Brielynn Jarvis, Jon Jarvis, Pastor Chris Johnson, Becca Lee, Nicole Lee, Amy Jo Mann, Candice Marino, Nikki McCauley, Angel Metzger, Lauren Mitchell, Jamie Powell, Maegan Roper, Doella Thomas, and Karla Thrasher. A huge thanks to Andy Rogers, my developmental editor. He helped me turn what sounded like a journal into a book that reads like a book. I will be forever grateful. Janelle Deblaay, thank you for going line by line and correcting mistakes made by a girl who can't even send a text without a misspelled word.

Lastly but not least importantly in any way, I need to thank all the aspiring writers that attended the writing workshop at the Oaks Retreat Center in November of 2022. Each of you made me feel like I belonged in the writing space. To Bob Goff, Kimberly Stuart, and the rest of the team, thank you for giving me the practical tips to make this book a reality, and for pouring gas on the fire within me. I couldn't have done this without each of you! I pray for all of you that, "The Lord bless you and keep you; the Lord make his face shine on you and be gracious to you; the Lord turn his face toward you and give you peace."[48]

Notes

1. www.usafacts.org/articles/how-many-kids-are-in-foster-care/.

2. www.nfyi.org/51-useful-aging-out-of-foster-care-statistics-social-race/.

3. www.adoptuskids.org.

4. (NIV).

5. John 21:15-16.

6. Matt. 6:28-30.

7. Matt. 14:13-21.

8. Luke 10:25-37.

9. "Foster Care: State vs. Private Agencies," Wait No More, Focus on the Family, last modified 2022, accessed, https://www.waitnomore.org/foster-care-state-vs-private-agencies/.

10. Isa. 58:11.

11. Rebecca St. James, vocalist, "Wait For Me," by Rebecca St. James, MP3 audio, track 8 on Transform, ForeFront Records, 2000.

12. Isa. 40:31.

13. John 14:6.

14. Matt. 7:1 (King James Version).

15. (NIV).

16. Bob Goff, these notes taken during the 2023 tour called "Bob Goff and Friends."

17. Heb. 13:8.

18. James 1:17.

19. TobyMac, vocalist, "Help Is on the Way," by TobyMac, YouTube Music, track 1 on Life After Death, ForeFront Records, 2022, https://www.youtube.com/watch?v=aVgetIvEIAs.

20. Isaiah 61:3.

21. Matt. 11:29.

22. Exodus 3:12.

23. Isaiah 55:9.

24. Lam. 3:22-24.

25. (NIV).

26. Gen. 39:21.

27. Gen. 42:8.

28. Gen. 44:33.

29. Jer. 29:11.

30. (NIV)

31. Corrie Ten Boom, Elizabeth Sherill, and John Sherill, The Hiding Place (Grand Rapids, MI: Chosen Books, 2006) xx.

32. Matt. 14:28.

33. Matt. 14:29.

34. Deut. 31:6.

35. 1 Samuel 3:9-10.

36. Bishop T.D. Jakes, "Feeding the Dream," Bishop T.D. Jakes 05/26/2015 May 26, 2015, video, 53:35, http://www.wordofyeshua.eu/feeding-the-dream/.

37. Charlotte Gamble, "Who Are You in Line For?" 03/01/15 March 1st 2015, video, 44:13, 1 https://www.churchofthehighlands.com/media/who-are-you-in-line-for.

38. Mark 5:21-43.

39. Exod. 14:27-29.

40. Most children age out of the foster care system at the age of 18, but 23 states allow the children to stay until 21 years of age unless the child asks to be emancipated-freed. Alabama is one of the 23 states that allow a longer stay.

41. Psalm 121:4.

42. Phil. 4:8.

43. Ps. 77:14.

44. Heb. 12:2.

45. Proverbs 13:12.

46. Gen. 32:22-32.

47. Jonah 1:17-3:2.

48. Nmbrs. 6:24-26.

www.ingramcontent.com/pod-product-compliance
Lightning Source LLC
Chambersburg PA
CBHW020234130626
46549CB00005B/1886